Donald R. Hands and Wayne L. Fehr

Spiritual Wholeness for Clergy

A New Psychology of Intimacy with God, Self and Others

with a foreword by Susan Howatch

A Publication of the Alban Institute

Library of Congress Catalog Card Number 92-75726
ISBN 1-56699-107-2

In memory of
Michael J. Stolpman
priest and visionary
founder of Saint Barnabas Center
1939-90

I am finally understanding just the tip of the iceberg about what the Resurrection means . . . I'm talking about the Resurrection as it applies to each of us. It means coming up through what you were born into, then understanding objectively the people your parents were and how they influenced you. Then finding out who you yourself are, in terms of how you carry forward what they put in you, and how your circumstances have shaped you. And then . . . and then . . . now here's the hard part! And then you have to slough off your "original sin," in the sense you defined it . . . You have to go on to find out what you are in the human drama, or body of God. The what beyond the who, so to speak.

—*Father Melancholy's Daughter*, Gail Godwin

CONTENTS

FOREWORD

This important book, focusing on an area where Christianity and psychology meet, reflects the growing realization that science and religion are not, as is still often thought, implacably opposed to each other, but are complementary aspects of a multi-sided truth. As Donald Hands and Wayne Fehr write of the spiritual journey and its psychological components, they clearly show that Christianity and psychology can mirror each other in describing the great human quest for self-realization and integration—or, in other words, the great call from God to fulfill his purpose by becoming the people he created us to be.

It is in this context that the authors write about the problems which can afflict the clergy, but because the clergy are on the road we are all called to travel, the authors' findings are of value to clergy and lay people alike. The message is one of hope. At the St. Barnabas Center the authors have been able to help distressed clergy along the way to recovery and renewal—a resurrection after the crucifixion of breakdown—by combining the techniques of psychotherapy with the wisdom of the Christian tradition. The medieval Christian mystics put great stress on the spiritual importance of knowing oneself in order to overcome sin, draw close to God and embark on the journey towards that state of completeness known in religious language as "eternal life." The modern psychotherapists also believe in the importance of self-knowledge; in facing up to past pain which has been suppressed and in acknowledging the shadow side of their personalities, the patients become empowered to win the battle against the self-destructive impulses that create despair and to set out on a new journey towards that state of wholeness known in psychotherapeutic language as "integration."

The authors expand on this example of how the healing steps of psychotherapy echo the spiritual explorations of the Christian mystical tradition. Dr. Hands and Dr. Fehr talk of "uncovery," "discovery," and "recovery" as they describe their patients' journeys out of darkness into light; the mystics talk of the "purgative," the "illuminative" and the "unitive" ways as they describe the pilgrim's progress towards God. The language changes but the human experience being described remains the same: it is the search to discover how we should live in order to be fully human, more wholly ourselves, finding lasting fulfillment in an honest and increasingly intimate relationship not only with those around us but with God.

While the authors were working with their distressed clergy and acquiring the wisdom which enabled this book to be written, I was embarking on a series of six novels about the Church of England in the twentieth century. Thousands of miles away on another continent, in complete ignorance of the work being done at the St. Barnabas Center, I found myself writing not only about the two languages which described the great Christian themes of redemption, resurrection, and renewal, but also about the spiritual journey of clergy who had lost their way.

When I began the project I knew no clergy well, but the more I began to empathize with my leading characters, the more clearly I saw that as clergymen they were people who had to live behind a professional facade which would impose considerable demands on their mental and emotional health. This problem was unpleasantly familiar to me, for as a commercially successful novelist I had come to feel early in the 1980s that I was stifled by a marketing image which bore increasingly little relation to my true self. Drawing on my own experience of how easy it is to become imprisoned by a false self—trapped behind a "glittering image"—I became more determined than ever to reject the idealized clerical stereotype, so commonly held by the laity, and portray my characters as real people, capable, just as we all are, of sinning not because they wanted to be wicked but because they were in some vital way cut off from God and alienated from their true selves.

However, the idea that the clergy could be fallible human beings proved shocking to many lay people, and it was left to a clergyman to exclaim to me eventually: "Thank God someone's finally telling it like it is!" That was when I realized I had touched on a reality that needed to be not denied with horror but explored with compassion, and that in turn was why I was so excited later to receive a letter from Donald Hands, telling me about his work at the St. Barnabas Center.

By acknowledging the dangers inherent in a clerical career and giving hope of renewal to those who have found those dangers overwhelming, the authors of *Spiritual Wholeness for Clergy* are also "telling it like it is," liberating those trapped behind a false facade and estranged from their true selves. This book would have been enormously valuable to the clerical central characters in my current series of novels: Charles Ashworth in *Glittering Images*, Jon Darrow in *Glamorous Powers*, and Neville Aysgarth in *Ultimate Prizes*—all of whom encounter a life crisis which shakes them to their foundations but which gives them the chance to redeem the past and go forward into the future to serve God far more effectively than they did before.

But perhaps Jon Darrow's son Nicholas is the character who would have most appreciated *Spiritual Wholeness for Clergy*. In the fifth of my novels about the church, *Mystical Paths*, he explores the synthesis of Jungian psychology and Christianity as developed by the late Anglican priest, monk, and spiritual director, Christopher Bryant. I believe Father Bryant would have welcomed this book by Donald Hands and Wayne Fehr. I can warmly recommend it not only to the clergy and those connected with them, but to all those committed to the search for self-realization and integration, to the service of God in the journey towards eternal life.

Susan Howatch

ACKNOWLEDGMENTS

We wish to acknowledge our debt of gratitude to our colleagues at the St. Barnabas Center, especially Rosita Torres, Mary Garke, and John Peterson. It has been in our collaboration that we have come to understand both the patterns of unhealth and the ways of healing. We are indebted also to the many men and women who have been patients at St. Barnabas. Their trust in us and their readiness to explore their own pain have enabled us to grow in understanding and skill. In all this learning, we recognize the mystery of God's providence.

INTRODUCTION

This book comes out of the authors' clinical experience with clergy in crisis in a treatment program that consciously and deliberately integrates spirituality and psychotherapy. From a variety of Christian denominations, men and women, named by different titles (priest, pastor, minister, brother, sister), have come to us in times of great personal and professional need. They came because they had reached a crisis, a breakdown point, and could no longer function.

Over a period of five years at the Saint Barnabas Center in Wisconsin we have worked intensively with these people in an inpatient treatment setting, where the average length of stay has been some five weeks. More than four hundred patients from various church traditions have opened to us the stories of their lives. Out of this rich, detailed clinical material we have gradually derived an understanding of the disorders from which many working clergy suffer.

Pathology and Healing

As they went through treatment for various disorders (substance addiction, compulsivity, depression, burnout, etc.), we became privileged witnesses of the pathology and pain in the lives of these dedicated church leaders. We came to understand the conditioning factors in their families of origin that made them vulnerable to emotional disorders.

We also came to understand the dynamics of healing and "recovery," as we worked intensively with so many patients. Across a variety of diagnoses and problems, we could discern a striking commonality in the process of healing.

As we strove to integrate the psychological and the spiritual in a wholistic model of therapy, we also saw that a radical spiritual conversion was at the heart of recovery for our patients. They could not begin to get well without entering into their relationship with God at a new depth of intimacy and surrender.

This primacy of the spiritual in their recovery shows us that what clergy need above all today is a genuine "personal spirituality." That is, they need to find a concrete way of living their relationship to God, so as to maintain a balance and integration of head and heart, work and leisure, intimacy and sexuality, prayer and action, professional role and personal life. In effect, they need to achieve a psychologically healthy spirituality.

An Ideal of Health

Somewhat paradoxically, it is out of our work with unhealthy and "dysfunctional" clergy that we are now able to derive an ideal of clergy health. We have learned about health from working with the unhealthy and seeing how they find healing. As we see what these men and women must do to become healthy and functional, we get some idea of the main features of a healthy way of life for clergy in our culture.

While we have been working with men and women in crisis, most of whom are quite unhealthy, what we have learned about the dangers, traps, and typical pathologies of working clergy now puts us in a position to write a book for all clergy, including those who are still relatively healthy. The argument, moreover, is addressed not only to clergy themselves, but also to all those whose lives and work are closely involved with clergy. In fact, the rich insights derived from working with clergy seem applicable also to a more general population, perhaps especially to other "helping professionals."

Relevance of this Material

In a world full of woes, why focus on the personal needs of clergy? Is a book like this an example of the typically North American preoccupation with the psychological well-being of the individual? Does it belong to the narcissistic culture of "feeling good?"

We are concerned to locate this specialized study in the much larger context of the church's mission to a suffering world. Both clergy and laity are called to a wider concern than their own personal health and well-being. They are called to bear witness to the power and love of God by working for justice, peace, and the total well-being of all humankind.

This mission to the entire human family and the future of the planet is an enormous challenge to all the churches today. To be faithful to this divine summons will require the best energies and deepest spirituality we can find. And it is our clergy who inevitably bear a large responsibility for the enlivening, strengthening, and inspiration of the entire Body, as they labor to "equip the saints for ministry" (Eph. 4:12).

On the other hand, it is no secret that many of our clergy today are, in various ways, "in trouble." The more sensational stories are picked up by the media. Many more men and women struggle privately, as they try to be faithful. And even those who are relatively healthy live with enormous stresses and burdens.

It is, therefore, clear that our clergy need help, care, and support. But helping the clergy to find greater emotional and spiritual well-being is not a matter merely of helping those individuals. Because of their key role in the life of the church, working for their health is really a ministry of the church to itself. For their health will have a healing and enlivening influence on all the communities they serve.

Moreover, to the extent that these clergy "in recovery" are living lives deeply open to the Spirit, they are also bound to become agents of the church's growing conversion to its responsibility for the world. In this way, the self-care of individuals can and must lead to their self-investment in the mission of the church to the world.

Method

The primary source of this book is our concrete clinical experience. The argument we present is grounded in the specifics of this empirical material. On the other hand, we necessarily draw upon theoretical resources to provide categories of interpretation. A context of meaning is provided from general principles of psychology, spirituality, and theology.

The method is also cross-disciplinary, in that one of the authors is a psychologist/clinician, while the other is a theologian/spiritual director.

Both are Episcopal priests. We have been working together in close collaboration from the very beginning of the Saint Barnabas program and have done our thinking and writing in constant dialogue and interaction.

Overview of Contents

The first two chapters provide the clinical background material out of which our argument is to be developed. Chapter I deals with the pathologies we have encountered, and Chapter II with the phases of the healing process as we see it take place. In presenting and explaining this material, we also introduce categories and themes basic to the development of the later chapters.

Beginning with Chapter III, then, we present a positive model for emotional and spiritual health—having in mind especially the situation of clergy in our present American culture. The content of these later chapters has to do, in various ways, with the notion of intimacy. We are convinced that the experience of intimacy is the core of health and salvation. Where intimacy is nurtured and experienced, there is no room for addictiveness and compulsivity.

Chapter III considers the theme of intimacy with oneself. Often neglected by clergy, this attitude of awareness and appreciation of self is crucial for healthy living. Without it, the clergyperson especially is almost inevitably drawn into a pattern of people pleasing and compulsive helping of others to fill an internal void.

Chapter IV considers the theme of intimacy with other persons. Emotionally close and honest relationships are essential to healthy living, but clergy are often emotionally isolated and self-contained as they strive to be all things to all people, to bless and comfort without themselves being known intimately and loved by others. Trying to live without interpersonal intimacy, they are vulnerable to various kinds of addiction. Learning to live in intimacy with others is essential to recovery and a psychologically healthy spirituality.

Chapter V considers the mystery that must be at the heart of a healthy way of life for clergy—intimacy with God. Despite a clergyperson's explicit commitment to nurture the faith-life of a community, his or her own personal spirituality may not be taken for granted. It needs to be pursued consciously and sustained by spiritual disciplines

and the support of peers. Paradoxically, the pressures of providing for
the spiritual needs of others can often work against the health and growth
of the minister's own spiritual life.

Chapter VI provides a summary and synthesis of the material
developed in the earlier chapters, with some practical recommendations
that arise from the argument.

CHAPTER I

The Deformation Process: Disorder

We begin with an account of the human condition as we have encountered it in our work—both its potential for health and its actual patterns of unhealthiness. The insights we have gained are both psychological and spiritual, so that we necessarily interweave the language of the clinician with that of the theologian and spiritual director.

Child of God

We find, first of all, a striking parallel between a widespread concept of current popular psychology and an equally familiar religious concept of the Christian tradition.

The concepts *inner child, child-within, true self,* etc., occur frequently in literature of the recovery movement and in popular psychological writings. In clinical practice, patients who suffer from childhoods lost to abuse and incest are given stuffed toys to hold and cuddle. These transitional objects serve as a bridge between their continuingly self-abused adult lives and the neglected, other-abused child-within. The contemporary adult self still acts as both perpetrator and victim, continuing the cycle with addictiveness or other pathology. The stuffed transitional object serves as a reified inner-child, so the adult person can now experience giving to that inner child the care that was not given originally or later.

From this perspective of the recovery movement, we can appreciate a familiar scriptural phrase "child of God" with a new sensitivity and depth. The prologue of John's gospel speaks of the power (literally, the "dynamic") that God gives us to become God's children (John 1:12-13).

The possibility of a new kind of birth or existence is proclaimed as Good News: One need not remain a victim of one's past or parenting. A *process* is hinted at—"to become"—and this is viewed as a gift from a Higher Power. By this divinely given dynamic, one can become a separate person in one's own right—not only the child of a particular set of parents, but a "child of God," a child that God intended from before one's birth.

We see in this text a genuine convergence with some of the best insights of the recovery movement. The phrases *inner child* and *true self* can be correlated with this Johannine sense of "child of God." Throughout this book, we will also be using another phrase to express the same truth: *what God intended*, that is, the original destiny of the human person in the mind and heart of God as revealed in God's Word, in the example of Christ, and in human experience.

By this usage, we are consciously acknowledging the mystery at the heart of human existence—that what we only gradually become, over years of growing, suffering, and learning, is known and willed from all eternity by the One who calls us into being. What is last in the order of accomplishment is actually first in the order of intention. That is, *God's* intention. And we ourselves discover most fully what we have always been intended to be, only at the end of all our journeying.

What God originally "intends" for us is not our addictiveness or compulsivity, not our personality disorders and defects, but the achievement of intimacy—with self, with others, and with God.

Despite the deformation that has occurred through the particular and peculiar kind of parenting each one has received, there is still the possibility of achieving the intended destiny of intimacy. This comes about through a healing process described in Chapter II.

This is the good news for the needy: John's prologue proclaims that the possibility, power, or dynamic to become a "child of God" is a *gift* from God that does not depend on the human bloodline or our human genealogy with its generational deficits and deformities.

Despite a person's victimizations, abuse, compulsions, or addictions, despite even the very vandalizing of the self in incest—it is possible, through struggle, pain, and the healing process, to recover that child intended by God in creation. We can bear witness to this kind of marvelous transformation in the lives of patients and parishioners and indeed, if we are not impostors, in our own lives as well.

Original Sin

As we consider how each person's becoming is both enabled and distorted by a family of origin, we find another parallel between the clinical
perspective and the faith-view of Christianity. The term that allows the
correlation is *original sin.*

This complex and controversial theological concept can perhaps be
understood in a fresh way in the light of the clinical data. We see it as a
way of expressing the weakness, the proclivity toward unhealth, and the
tendency toward behaviors destructive to self or others that plague every
human being. More than that, it also connotes an origin of this unhappy
condition that preexists any free choices of the individual. So, the concept may be helpful for referring to the "embeddedness" of human freedom in a familial and social matrix that enables, conditions, and distorts
it.

In making use of this theological concept, we wish to focus more on
the word *original* than on *sin. Sin* is here to be regarded compassionately
as woundedness, not judgmentally as moral fault, with culpability and
blaming. On the other hand, this understanding of original sin does not
deny personal responsibility for recovery from the sins of others against
us, especially the wounds received from parenting. Although we have no
responsibility whatever for the original wounds received, we do have a
responsibility to recover from them as best we can.

The word *sin* has admittedly become problematic for many, as it
carries with it unfortunate associations of judgment, condemnation, and
rejection. Yet, we think the concept is still both valid and useful. Today's emphasis, to be sure, is away from "toxic shame" or "toxic guilt,"
that crippling sense of personal unworthiness that thwarts God's power
to transform.

The contemporary focus is often on "original blessing" (Fox, 1983)
rather than original sin. This is certainly a positive development insofar
as it helps undo the shame many people have been made to feel by their
church's historically heavy-handed, judgmental attitude, and its failure to
reach out and offer hope to those wounded by addictiveness and emotional disorder.

On the other hand, it is unrealistic to overlook or minimize the
negative legacy so many people receive from their families of origin.
The case histories of addicted and compulsive people make this shadow

side unmistakably evident. Hence, the concept of original sin still has some relevance, to maintain a balanced view of the human condition.

A well-known song characterizes the dilemma of addicted and compulsive people: "Looking for love in all the wrong places." We affirm, bless, and "unshame" the *search* for love or intimacy, but we stand against and condemn the "wrong places" of addictiveness—chemical, food-related, or sexual. These wrong places keep the inner child ever needy, ever empty, depressed, and a victim.

For example, we know that sexual addicts (or sexual compulsives or sexual dependents) generally come from families of origin that were both rigid and emotionally disengaged (Carnes, 1989). It appears that such people are still seeking the nurturance they did not experience growing up. They still hunger for that intimacy that was not provided or modeled when they were children.

Genital sexuality is a powerful counterfeit of interpersonal intimacy and is often abused as a drug of choice. We do not want to shame the need for intimacy, but we need to condemn the abuse of persons as objects for addictive needs. There is often, in fact, a transformation from victim to perpetrator of abuse—a deformed way of making up for the original deprivation. Though understandable, such a pattern of behavior is clearly unacceptable.

In recognizing the harm sometimes done to children by their families of origin, the point is not primarily to criticize or blame the parents. Rather, the important thing is to help people realize the hurts they have suffered and the prices they have paid for the wounds received. Most people in early recovery are too loyal to their parents to be able to name what was missing in their development. They readily excuse their parents' shortcomings and even abuses—but this defensiveness is a way of focusing away from their own pain.

Since this is the task most feared—to feel one's own pain—to tie this up with disloyalty is an effective maneuver against painful affect. The point is that, even though one's parents did not mean the harm they did, the child nevertheless did and still does hurt. We have, in fact, learned about parents who have inflicted terrible suffering on their children. These are extreme cases, but in such situations the concept of original blessing may seem trivial or unrealistically optimistic.

In this connection, it is sometimes asked how a child with no positive experience or memory of father can have any positive comprehension of the analogy of God as father. To such a person, the proclamation of God as father must seem baffling, purely wishful thinking, or enraging. Yet we believe that such a child still longs and yearns for a good and faithful father, even without actual experience. We believe we are dealing here with a deep longing of the human heart, a mystery in which the human still longs for what has never yet been actualized. There are images of abused children clinging to the feet of the abusing parent—pathetically longing to give the parent another chance.

When such abusive parents do not recover, their children in later life must emotionally disengage and look for the needed nurturance elsewhere. They must almost stop being the children of Mom X and Dad Y and become "children of God," looking for love and intimacy in all the *right* places.

The original wound, void, or emptiness has the possibility of being transformed into a window of opportunity, a spaciousness and a capacity for reaching out toward and connecting with others—a process of healing to be celebrated. Gerald May has written about this ever-present possibility (G. May, 1991).

Families of Origin: Two Patterns of Deformation

Two basic kinds of families of origin deform their children. The distinction between them has to do with boundaries, that space between persons that defines where each ends emotionally and physically. The notion of boundary is well expressed by Robert Bolt in his preface to *A Man for All Seasons* (1960), where he says that Thomas More had "an adamantine sense of his own self . . . He knew where he began and where he left off . . ." He had a well-defined set of boundaries, knew where he would have to yield, and where he would have to set like steel against the forces of his enemies.

The first kind of family that deforms its children violates the children's boundaries, crossing over the line physically, sexually, and/or emotionally. These parents are the abusers, the incest-perpetrators, the batterers, those who invade, vandalize, and brutalize. Such families are more obviously pathological than the other kind.

These are the families who have transformed personal boundaries into walls. They have built emotional barriers around themselves, obeying the so-called dysfunctional family triad: "Don't talk. Don't trust. Don't feel." Paradoxically, such families look good, appear strong and virtuous to the outside world. They are often cited and rewarded for their accomplishments. Many are regarded as pillars of their churches.

The popular concept of "dysfunction" may seem inappropriate as applied to such families. If anything, these families either overfunction or just barely function, in the sense of providing the basic physical needs of food and warm shelter. And they often produce high achievers.

This kind of parenting is often representative of the post-Depression-era cohort of parents. Their emphasis was on survival, materialism, and getting ahead. Literally, these families are quite functional, but their children are more like functionaries than intimate members who are confident of their basic belongingness.

These two kinds of families produce children with different kinds of wounds. Their responses and reactions are generally predictable and distinct.

Children whose boundaries have been violated tend toward some kind of rebellious hostility, either exploding their anger outward toward behaviors destructive to others or imploding their anger inward toward self-destructive acts.

Children whose boundaries were turned into walls are less manifestly angry but more emotionally empty, dependent, and needy, tending toward behaviors designed to placate and please others. They are prone to the whole host of traits that comprise the notion of _codependency_. Of course, life is rarely so easy to categorize, and most adults exhibit some combination of both rebellious and codependent features.

The Split: Dissociation of Affect from Cognition

In both kinds of families, feelings other than "glad" are neither allowed, tolerated, nor modeled. Feelings of sadness, hurt, anger, or fear are not expressed or even accessed. These natural human emotions are denied.

For an extreme though illustrative example, take the experience of child victims of sexual abuse or incest. In the moment of their assault, the children had to suppress their fear, terror, anger, and hurt to survive and ward off further danger. The hurt and felt woundedness had to be kept secret, often with threats of reprisal for any disclosure. Justifiable

anger was not available to the children at that time, needing to be repressed for safety and survival. In its stead, the children were left with
guilt and shame, believing that they were in some way culpable, defective. The children then believe that such natural feelings are either
wrong and not to be trusted or too dangerous to access, let alone express.
They begin to separate affect from cognition and to "shame" feelings
other than gladness.

A similar process of shaming basic and justified feelings occurs with
children from families with walls. Since few or no feelings were expressed, the very capacity and human endowment of affect became sus-
pect. Survivors of such families wonder if having feelings is normal or
not.

There is a joke about who is a "normal" person. The answer?
Anyone whom one doesn't know very well. Such humor is actually a
relief to adult children who feel abnormal and strange when they begin to
feel emotion for the first time, especially when the "first time" is in
midlife.

The walled-in families leave their children with the legacy of
"unlove." Understandably, children of such families tend to develop
addictions to sex and love or to become codependent.

The children of both these kinds of families develop a separation
between their affective and cognitive capacities. This split is defensive
and was necessary for survival.

Victims of severe abuse frequently dissociate—separate feelings
from thoughts, body from mind, perceptions from reality—to survive the
trauma of their assaults. For example, a girl being sexually assaulted
sees the scene from outside the window; it is not really happening to her,
only to the detached body in the bed.

In less extreme situations, or with children from walled-in families,
using one's head becomes the way to survive or to try to meet those
unmet needs for nurturance and intimacy. These children rechannel
needs for affection into needs for achievement, and this becomes never-
ending, a striving for more and more. Ultimately, such a project is
doomed. Achievements do not substitute for basic deficits in nurturance.

Unfortunately, society and seminaries almost exclusively reward the
achievements of the head and either ignore or presume the accomplishments of the heart. This is a sad situation, for, as we know from Scripture, the core of the person is the heart, not the head. In Aristotle's

definition of the human being as a "rational animal" (*zoon logikon*), the head or mind or intellect is the defining difference and the core of the person. Not so in Scripture, where the heart is the center and core. The heart is the locus of the core-beliefs as they develop from families of origin.

Children deprived of nurturance are often high achievers who use their heads to survive the developmental tasks of their twenties and early thirties. To leave home and get established financially and to create a family of one's own requires a good deal of cognitive effort. While engaged in these tasks, it isn't opportune or necessary to explore or access one's affective life. Paradoxically, we see many highly educated persons who are unable to access and name their basic feelings.

Facing One's Pain

What begins the healing process, in terms of closing the gap between the cognitive and affective domains, is simply and profoundly the felt experience of one's own pain. On the other hand, what maintains that separation of head and heart is addictiveness, compulsivity, or other types of emotional disorder. Addictions and compulsions are what one does instead of allowing oneself to experience the pain.

One can complete the blocked process by experiencing the never-mourned, original hurts, grief, losses, fear, or anger as felt by the child (now the inner child) in a safe place. This natural emotional process of arousal and expressive discharge was interrupted by the cycle of abuse and by the continuing adult addictive processes. Such natural feelings were shamed and repressed long ago but remain dynamic and alive within the core of the person.

What prevents their access, expression, taming, and healing is the compulsive/addictive processes that try to keep life at controllable and predictable levels. Dissociated individuals attempt to explain everything away while maintaining a numbed affective development.

Clergy-Specific Dysfunction

There are some distinctive characteristics of the religious professional's attempt to maintain the cognitive-affective separation. The "facade" of such a person results from the attempt to present only a highly rational, intellectualized, and even morally superior front.

The recovery literature has identified a number of roles learned in dysfunctional families: the hero, the scapegoat, the clown, and the lost child. These roles are adopted and learned by children to survive in the family of origin, whether violent or walled-in.

Clergy tend to fall into two of these roles: the hero or the clown (mascot). Seldom do we encounter a scapegoat, except in the cases of clergy who are sociopathic and out to "con" people. And the lost child usually does not manage to complete a graduate-level education.

The hero is almost a given role, near axiomatic, even archetypal, for clergy. The hero fixes others, achieves status in the community, and focuses energies and affect on the problems of others. The hero works long hours, skips vacations, or if on vacation is bored and restless. The hero is well trained to run away from the emptiness or loneliness that might be uncovered during "time off"; it is better to keep working. This culminates in the "Messiah complex" (R. May, 1938), the hero's delusion that his or her efforts are both supremely ordained and indispensable for others' health and salvation. Clerical heroes are ambitious, not necessarily in the materialistic or power sense, but in their belief that they can manage and handle a dozen or more projects or committees at once.

Some dysfunctional families of origin may feel blessed, even vindicated, when a son or daughter enters the professional ministry as an ordained or vowed person. In the past, this may have been especially true among some Roman Catholics. *We must have done something right, or God wouldn't have blessed us with a vocation.* This thinking is a device to minimize, rationalize, or justify whatever pain and suffering were inflicted on the child.

This dynamic is illustrated in the case of an adult survivor of severe parental physical abuse and fraternal incest who became a priest. As is not uncommon, he had left home for preseminary at an early adolescent age, to escape the abusive family. Whenever he would return home for the sporadic family reunion, his parents, siblings, and entire extended family would fall to their knees for his priestly benediction. Incidentally, it is tragic that the religious training institutes that have taken such candidates, even at such an early age, ordinarily have not addressed the person's past woundedness until a severe crisis occurs.

In summary, the hero's emotional resources and repertoire for ministry are quite limited, centering on mechanisms of denial and limited to feelings of gladness or a bland "chronic niceness."

The other role assumed by future church professionals is that of the clown. This is the mascot or entertainer role of the one who tries hard to divert attention from the abuse, neglect, or lack of love in the family. The clown, trying to please the inadequate parent or abuser, is well-versed in the ways of getting attention and placating others. The clown's attention, like the hero's, is directed toward others—but to make them laugh and to keep everyone smiling.

The clown's emotions are also limited to the one tolerated feeling: gladness. Clowns are conflict-avoidant, even to the point of phobia. When someone begins to access or express a feeling other than gladness, such as grief, fear, hurt, or anger, the clown tells a joke or makes a cute remark. The diversionary tactic is painfully obvious to all who listen, and the clown gets a goodly share of pity more than genuine laughter.

Clowns become chronically nice, and this blandness is unfortunately often equated with virtue. This niceness becomes a social norm for ministry and develops into pathogenic proportions. Such placating clergy tend to burn out, exhausted by the energy required to stay "nice" and therefore keep repressed all the other natural feelings forbidden in the family of origin.

The pathogenic process continues when the church community is as dysfunctional as the family of origin. Clowns are easy prey to depressions, as they pretend everything is all right when down deep they know it isn't. They are performers and, in a sense not yet available even to their conscious awareness, impostors.

Developmental Aspects

These facades or public masks survive through the twenties and thirties, the decades of external activity and accomplishment. Jung calls this time the morning of life (Jung, 1971). He cautions us not to try to live in the afternoon of life, i.e., midlife, according to the principles of the morning. From this perspective, it is not surprising that the clergy who break down do so most often in midlife.

By this time some degree of external success has been achieved—maybe school completed, degrees earned, mortgage and housing provided, marriage and children on the way. The repressed affects often surface in surprising and sometimes dramatic ways in midlife because by this time a person is strong enough to face the unresolved issues of the past. By midlife, also, a person's well-maintained facade may delude him or her into thinking he or she can face these unresolved issues alone and resolve them with rational, problem-solving techniques.

Susan Howatch has captured in a sweeping, epic manner the ways and waywardness of clergy in her novels about the Church of England. Six novels make up the series, and the first's title, *Glittering Images* (1987), speaks of the felt need to maintain or manage images—facades— on both a personal and institutional level. Her clergy refrain from cigarettes only when wearing clerical collars, buy condoms in secular dress in cities where they are not recognized. They even refrain from full intercourse with penile penetration, but enjoy mutual orgasm in the name of not technically committing adultery.

As a novelist she is able to portray from the inner heart the conflicts caused for clergy by such discrepancy between belief-systems and behaviors. The dissonance between the secret lives and the public presentations of self is her creative bailiwick, and she accomplishes a truly marvelous and compassionate work in exposing the costs of this to both clergy and church.

Jung's insights into the stages of life are apropos and a source of hope for those in midlife turmoil (Jung, 1971). In his sweeping vision of the human psychological life-span, there are three divisions of life, named journeys.

The first journey extends from physical birth to the death of the "false self" at midlife. The second journey begins with the process of healing the first journey's wounds and extends to the beginning of the third journey, which is the person's facing the more immediate challenges of dying. What this means is that the death of the first journey's "facade" is followed by a birth into a second journey—more authentic, genuine, and free than the first. In this second journey we are getting closer and closer to the original "child of God," the person intended from the beginning and from before creation.

No other developmental sequence presents such a vast expanse of time from birth to the death of the false self. Jung had a deep spiritual awareness, which explains such a panoramic vision of human life. The first journey extends through infancy, childhood, adolescence, young adulthood, and into midadulthood. It encompasses the time of the original woundedness in families of origin, survival mechanisms of repression, and the separation of cognition from affect, fed by addictiveness and our facades. Finally, emotional breakdown/breakthrough brings one to the brink of potential recovery of one's lost way.

This healing process often begins in the second journey, a time with increased vulnerability and openness to the promptings of the child-within. The dynamic is illustrated in the stories of saints who made radically new beginnings—Francis of Assisi, Teresa of Avila, and in our own days Mother Teresa of Calcutta.

Dante presents the midlife dilemma in the opening verses of the *Inferno*, which can be read allegorically as a journey of personal recovery —a journey down into the hell of one's past, parenting, and woundedness.

Dante begins his epic: "In the middle of the journey of my life I awaken and discover myself in a dark wood, and I am alone and afraid." To "awaken" suggests the process of uncovering the illusions of the past; to "discover" suggests learning the truth about oneself and one's history. These first two phases of the healing process prepare the way for the "recovery" of one's lost inner child, as we will argue in Chapter II.

It is noteworthy that Dante dares not make this journey alone but is accompanied by Virgil, who himself has already made the journey. Nor can one travel down into his or her personal and private hell all alone and hope to return unscathed. Either one will take a mind- or mood-altering substance as a companion (an intimacy-substitute) or, in the case of serious mental illness, invent an imaginary companion, as in the psychoses.

It is at the point where the long-maintained facade is breaking down that the staff of a treatment center meet a clergyperson as patient (and where, often enough, clergy meet troubled parishioners for counseling).

Persons in need of treatment or other pastoral help might be called symptomatic selves—so distressed, or the cause of so much distress, that some intervention becomes necessary.

At this entry point into the formal healing process, the troubled or troubling person does not know the meaning, extent, or source of the pain felt personally or inflicted on others. He or she wants relief above all, but is not usually ready or immediately willing to undergo profound personality change through radical cognitive and affective restructuring. Such change is resisted as unwelcome, undesirable, or even impossible.

So here the formal process often begins—with fear and trepidation, denial and doubt, confusion and anger.

Spiritual Aspects

This clinical survey would not be complete without considering also the *spiritual* condition of the symptomatic selves, the people whose facades have broken down.

Nearly all the clergy who have come to us for treatment of emotional disorders and/or addictions have also been suffering from a spiritual malaise. Many of them are at a point of estrangement from God, with scarcely any genuine personal relationship to the Mystery that they proclaim to others.

The spiritual condition of these patients is very closely related to the kinds of emotional unhealthiness surveyed in this chapter. In most of them we see a pattern of excessive and compulsive absorption in the work of ministry, to the neglect of personal needs and primary relationships. In their striving to please everyone in their surroundings, to take care of everyone's needs, and to avoid all conflict, they have become estranged from self, from the people closest to them, and from God. Their compulsive behaviors are recognizable as a poor substitute for intimacy and communion.

When asked to characterize their spiritual state, they tend to answer with phrases like "spiritual bankruptcy," "utter dryness," "emptiness." They feel the estrangement; they sense the absence of the reality of God from their conscious lives.

The dissociation of head and heart is especially noticeable in these clergy. They are well educated in theology, and are often eloquent in speaking of the truths of Christian faith. But they have either never felt deeply and personally the truths they proclaim, or they have gradually drifted away from a personal relationship to them.

The split between understanding and feeling is perpetuated by their failure to spend time regularly in personal prayer. For most, their prayer is almost exclusively public, intercessory, or linked with their ministry to others. They do not spend time in silent openness to God or let the Word of God speak to their own personal situations. Their flight from self-knowledge is inseparable from their avoidance of silent, personal encounter with God.

Consequently, they live with a sense of doubleness, aware of a painful and embarrassing contrast between what they preach to others and the way they live their own lives. This lack of integration causes feelings of dishonesty and hypocrisy, especially when these clergy exhibit patterns of addictive behavior.

Summary

Summing up the clinical findings of this chapter: We see the "child of God" born into a concrete and historical family situation. This situation leads to the development of a split, wounded, and false self that separates affect from cognition and denies woundedness. This false self is maintained by addictiveness and personality disorder that make the facade or public persona mandatory. But this false front lasts only so long: eventually it is no longer useful or necessary for survival and becomes unmasked in midlife. Then life circumstances and inner resources combine to provide a crisis/opportunity, a breakdown/breakthrough for the healing process to begin.

CHAPTER II

The Healing Process: Psychological and Ascetical Parallels

The preceding chapter provided an overview of the kinds of pathology and spiritual malaise that we have found in the clergy who have come to us for help. We turn now to the process of healing by which they gradually emerge from their unhappy condition.

We see the healing process as in some ways parallel to the classical ascetical journey of the heart's yearning for God. For centuries the three stages of that journey have been called the Via Purgativa, the Via Illuminativa, and the Via Unitiva—the purgative, illuminative, and unitive ways. Somewhat parallel to these stages of the spiritual life, we distinguish three phases of the process of healing. We will call these phases "uncovery," discovery, and recovery.

Looking at the person who comes to treatment, we need to ask: How can this person move out of emptiness and emotional isolation into a real relationship of intimacy with self, with other persons, and with God?

The process begins as one admits just how bad things have been. This is extremely difficult for anyone, but perhaps especcially for clergy because of their idealized self-image and their very high wall of defenses.

The Purgative Process of "Uncovery"

The first phase of healing may be called "uncovery," that is, the stripping away of the facade or public persona behind which the patient has been hiding the real disorder and pain of his or her life. This seems parallel to the purgative way in which one undergoes the painful process of recognizing and then ridding oneself of bad habits and sinful behaviors.

In our perspective, this cleansing and purging of false, unloving, hurtful actions and habits must go along with the recognition of false ways of thinking, feeling, and imagining. This usually includes distorted and oppressive images of God and forms of religiosity. All this needs to be uncovered and deprived of its power over us.

The uncovering often begins with the appearance or awareness and working-through of symptoms and/or the appearance of behavior that is uninvited and unwelcomed.

Symptoms are usually disconcerting; they shake a person out of the routine, business-as-usual patterns of life. They appear out of the crumbling of the false self, which can no longer carry the burden of maintaining the separation or split discussed in the previous chapter.

The manifestation of such symptoms precipitates a life-crisis that can also be an opportunity, even though it has not been sought and may not seem opportune.

For example, consider how "uncovery" came about in the life of a pastor who had relapsed with his alcoholism. Though he had completed a twenty-eight-day residential program, after half a year he stopped working his Alcoholics Anonymous program and began drinking again. He was neglecting his duties and trying to cover up his deficiencies. One cover-up tactic was lying to an elderly female parishioner whose memory was beginning to wane. He told her that he had visited her chronically incapacitated husband in a nursing home, when in fact he had not done so. She believed his lies and chalked up the confusion to her failing memory, more convinced than the facts warranted that her mental status was rapidly deteriorating.

For the pastor, a moment of "uncovery" came as he *uncovered* his lies and saw them for what they were; he was not the facade he presented. He was able to use this self-unmasking as a motivator for seeking help and readmittance to a rehabilitation program. When he uncovered his cruel manipulation of the parishioner, he broke through the pride-shame barrier that had been maintaining his facade.

It often takes a drastic event to get a person to face symptoms and seek treatment. This may come through the intervention of spouse and/ or colleagues and bishop. It may come through the disclosure of some misconduct. It may come through some health problem or in the form of a depression so severe that one can no longer function.

Even when such a person has come to treatment, a major and prolonged effort by the staff is often needed to break down the defenses and get the person to look squarely at what his or her life has really been like. There is often so much pain, so much harm to self and others, so much resentment ("frozen anger")—but all hidden behind the carefully maintained facade of the professional, competent, affable clergyperson. To whom can he or she admit the truth?

In the treatment setting, the patient is finally able to admit the truth of his or her life not only to the staff but also to fellow patients. The shame of such self-disclosure is gradually overcome by the continuing acceptance and respect shown to the person by peers and staff. It is a great relief when the secrets are out, when the worst is known, and one finds oneself still in relationship with the others, still a member of the one Body, still loved.

Working through symptoms is, to be sure, purgative in the sense that it hurts and stings to have one's defenses broken down or broken through. What mitigates this pain is the felt experience of a caring though confrontative and challenging community. Group settings where feedback can be given and solicited serve this purpose.

Pastors and priests do not ordinarily receive much genuine, regular, or adequate feedback and are often left unaware of their blind spots (what is known to others but unknown to self) and their actual impact on others.

Clergy tend and want to believe that, because their intentions are good, their impact on others is also good. This attitude is a professional and personal shortcoming since clergy—as persons and as religious professionals—are responsible for the impact of their actions as well as for their intentions. Nowhere does this become more problematic than in the area of sexual boundaries.

For example, the matter of clergy giving hugs to parishioners is currently controversial in light of sexual abuse and boundary issues. For a particular clergyman, an unsolicited hug given to a female parishioner may have the best of intentions, meaning to express warmth, kindness, or condolence. To a particular recipient, however, it may be a frightening experience, especially if she has had her physical and sexual boundaries violated in the past. In such a situation the clergyman needs to respect the woman's boundaries and, if there is any doubt, ask if she wants a hug.

In the setting of a trusted community, where negative and challenging feedback can be solicited and given, clergy can be made aware of their blind spots. Though painful, such challenging feedback is easier to accept because of the concern and caring of the community in a treatment setting.

In summary, the first phase of the healing process, "uncovery," is a movement from the appearance of symptoms to a disclosure of what one's life is actually like behind the carefully honed image. This stinging and sometimes bitter process parallels the purgative way, the first stage of the heart's journey toward the final object of its yearning.

The Illuminative Process of Discovery

The second stage of that movement is the illuminative way, the process by which the soul is enlightened and consoled by glimpses and discoveries of the Divine Reality. This kind of learning is not merely intellectual but involves a "conversion" of the whole person—imagination, feelings, desires, behavior, as well as understanding. The "light" in question illuminates and thereby transforms all the dimensions of being human. In general, one could speak of a growth in "wisdom," which includes one's ways of imagining and relating to God.

There is a certain parallel here with the second phase of healing, which we call discovery—the way of learning and accepting the truth about one's own life. Light is gradually shed on what previously has been dark, unknown, or unprocessed.

This involves the process of looking inward—behind the mask— and downward or backward, as it were, to one's roots in the family of origin. This discovery can be painful at first, but when one's defects are seen in the light of contributory though not exculpatory background, then a possibility emerges of both self-understanding and self-forgiveness.

The process of discovery may be illustrated in the case of some pastors who, having repressed their past adolescent victimization, perpetrate ephebophilic sexual abuse. (The term is a Greek derivative for "sexual attraction to adolescent males.") Healing discovery occurs when they can see themselves as having turned into the very kinds of monsters who molested them in their younger years. After their own abusive behavior has been uncovered, they often recall their own past victimization. As they uncover repressed anger and outrage at those who molested them, they discover their own tragic victim-to-perpetrator transformation. The moments of this discovery are often dramatic, heart-wrenching, and healing.

In such cases, it is typically not they themselves who uncover their abusive behaviors, but others, often their current victims or the victims' parents. Here "uncovery" occurs by virtue of exposure, not by voluntary disclosure; they have been caught and denounced.

The moment of discovery, however, comes when they can personally understand and feel the pain of a negative self-transformation process through which they had become the very objects of their past hatreds, now acting as subjects and agents of abuse against others. Further discovery comes as they develop an empathy for their victims, enhanced by the grieving process of mourning their own victimization and losses.

The Unitive Process of Recovery

The third phase of healing is the process of recovery, which connotes the regaining of what was lost, the restoration of the "child of God," becoming more and more of what God originally intended. This is parallel to the unitive way in which the soul's growing union with God through love brings about its ever increasing transformation into the image and likeness of God.

In this context of meaning, the notion of "being in recovery" has a truly spiritual quality. For clergy especially, *being in recovery* can have a rich, integrated meaning, whereby the emotional processes of "uncovery," discovery, and recovery are seen to be parallel with the phases of spiritual growth and transformation.

It should be noted that the phrase *in recovery,* with its connotation of being in an ongoing process, is in deliberate contrast with the term *recovered.* It is generally recognized that there is no "cure" for addictions, or, for that matter, for any of our tendencies toward various forms of disorder, such as depressions or anxieties. The proclivities will always stay with us. We will always tend toward some individual, highly personalized types of potential problems. We remain ever vulnerable to unique weaknesses or tendencies toward disorder, defects, and distress.

There are, however, ways of coping with and managing one's ailments. People are powerless over their unique proclivities toward problems but are not helpless in using appropriate tools and skills to prevent actualization of their tendencies.

Alcoholics, for example, are powerless over their disease and the ways their bodies react to the chemical, but they are not helpless to prevent the taking of that first drink. There is a way to manage the impulse to do that; for many, it is the way of life of the Twelve Steps.

Alcoholics and the rest of us who are broken in other ways are never fully cured or recovered. Rather, to be "in recovery" is a life-long process. This is especially true since recovery demands that one work to build a lifestyle that helps prevent turning to various disorders or addictive processes for relief of pain.

To restore what was lost, that originally intended "child of God," is, therefore, never fully attainable or finished in this life. In this sense, too, living "in recovery" parallels the unitive way. This last of the three journeys of the heart involves the ever closer communion of the heart with the object of its desire, God. Such communion in this life is most perfectly described by the mystics as a "union" or even as a "marriage," but to be made more and more perfect in the next life. The unitive way describes a relationship that is never totally finished but is always to be deepened.

Affective Healing

The three phases of the healing process may also be regarded in terms of feelings. In dysfunctional families of origin, as we have seen, some feelings were shamed out of awareness; others were never allowed to be expressed; others were punished severely. They have become repressed or buried, numbed or anesthetized. Feelings other than some kind of gladness were labeled "bad" or "negative" and disowned. It was not safe to feel these repressed feelings.

De-repression of feelings is an important aspect of the first phase of the healing process. As a matter of survival, the child learned to repress or suppress specific feelings such as sadness, hurt, anger, or fear or to ignore the affective life totally in favor of the more cognitive aspects. The first phase of healing, therefore, involves the "uncovery" of these shamed affects.

The healing process for feelings continues as the person learns where to direct and focus the feelings now experienced or uncovered. This is the affective discovery process. A caring community is experienced as a safe place not only to access (uncover) but also to *express* feelings directly and in a focused way toward the original significant others whose words and deeds aroused such powerful feelings in the first place.

This involves a struggle as the person must also discover that the ownership and targeted expression of these feelings is not disloyalty toward those original significant ones. Both anger and love can coexist in healthy relationships. True loyalty to another, and the most respectful gesture one can make toward another, is to share feelings honestly and appropriately.

In the safety of a caring community, affect is loosened: Tears begin to be shed; anger surfaces; grief is vented; shame is broken through. The person recovers the affective life he or she had to abandon to survive in childhood. Since that early splitting-off of the affective life had facilitated the development of the facade and the addictive/compulsive problems, an adult recovers the lost "child" as he or she learns to access and express feelings. In this way the inner split is healed.

What Is Uncovered and Discovered

What are the characteristics of the uncovered self, the hidden side of the person behind the facade or public presentation? We can generalize some findings. Remove the mask and you see aspects of the person that were shamed into hiddenness. "If you knew these things about me, you wouldn't like me anymore" is the expressed feeling of the people who manage their images carefully. The following is what we often find behind the false self and the symptomatology.

Typically, fear is uncovered. This fear can be divided into two kinds, both of which interfere with the capacity for intimacy. The two types of fear relate to the two kinds of deforming families of origin described in Chapter I.

On the one hand, there is the fear (felt especially by men) of enmeshment, that is, the emotional equivalent of being swallowed up by another person, losing one's autonomy and even identity. Intimacy is impossible under these conditions. The price of drawing close to another is equated with the loss of self.

When someone's boundaries have been violated, as in the physically or sexually abusing family, to become emotionally close to another

person is dangerous and threatening. When emotional abuse has occurred in the original family, the price of closeness has been experienced
as having to do the powerful parent's bidding. Closeness is equated
experientially with loss of independence and autonomy.

On the other hand, there is the fear (felt especially by women) of
abandonment, the experience of being left or rejected. The child feels
this as equivalent to annihilation. Families who have made boundaries
into walls, who keep members emotionally isolated from one another,
contribute to the person's feeling and fear of being abandoned. This fear
can predominate in interpersonal relationships and leads to the whole
host of disorders connoted by the term *codependency*.

Both fears debilitate the capacity and readiness for intimacy. Those
afraid of enmeshment are often angry people who alienate others to
maintain the safe distance required if they are not to lose autonomy.
They can also be controlling, domineering types. On the other hand,
those afraid of abandonment are often dependent and people-pleasers.

"Heroes," often fearing enmeshment, prefer to fix others; taking on
the dominant role of helper or therapist, they are the ones giving to
others. On the other hand, "clowns" fear abandonment and will placate
others to keep relationships alive despite the cost.

Another uncovered characteristic is a sense of emptiness or of a
painful void. Some describe it as a constant companion, an inner ache or
sorrow. For some it is almost palpable, a felt lack that some trace back
to a never-experienced, missing sense of original touch or nurturance.
There is a feeling of deprivation and a despair of ever being able to
eliminate the void or feel an inner peace or wholeness.

Many maneuvers and symptoms are developed to cover up this
painful void. We witness this with those who abuse alcohol or drugs or
other substances or processes. Alcohol, drugs, food, sex, control, or
codependency are used to fill this emptiness.

It is a pity that the alcoholic often cannot develop an intimate relationship with another person. We believe that all addicts, regardless of
the various objects of their addictiveness, attach themselves to their
drugs of choice as substitutes for intimacy. Objects of addiction seem
more predictable and more easily controlled than other persons. They
usually provide their relief or mood change and make one feel good,
while persons cannot be so reliable or so easily controlled at will.

Another characteristic that is uncovered when a facade and symptoms are unmasked is a failure of empathy. One realizes one's former inability to recognize another person as truly separate, rather than just an extension of oneself.

Addicts, for example, use people to fill themselves and their needs. This is quite true also of clergy involved in sexual boundary violations. Such clergy, typically men, cross over pastoral and professional boundaries and engage in sex with female parishioners. Often there is a pattern of such abuse throughout a person's ministry.

Such clergy are narcissistic, that is, they become so fixated on and preoccupied with their felt neediness and lack of nurturance that they rationalize and justify their violations of others' boundaries. Their needs have become demands and take on a coercive quality that gives them a sense of entitlement, a right to violate others.

Such empathic failures accompany and characterize most of the addictions and disorders we have mentioned. Whenever one's focus is fixated on personal lacks or needs, rights and prerogatives, entitlements and status, there is a real danger of empathic failure.

When uncovered, these characteristics can shock a person. The awareness of these defects stings and hurts. A process of de-illusionment is a part of growth and discovery. By this term, we mean coming to regard one's previous core-beliefs as inadequate or just plain wrong, or realizing that they were illusory.

This is not the same as disillusionment, which characterizes depression and despair, though the de-illusionment process can develop into disillusionment. This happens when a person is left to face illusions alone and without support. Then de-illusionment feels like abandonment and becomes overwhelming.

Shame

One other characteristic of the "uncovery" process is the recognition of shame as a basic core-belief. Shame has been phenomenologically described by Gershen Kaufman (1985). From his description of three moments of this most basic and soul-killing experience, it is not difficult to see how shame underpins the morbid processes we discussed in Chapter I.

Kaufman first identifies some kind of break or rupture of an interpersonal bond that should have been there. Witness the two kinds of families of origin we have been describing. Second, along with this break, one experiences a feeling of diminishment or unworthiness. This is more than guilt, which can be helpful. Guilt is when I admit I made a mistake, broke a rule or law, and get back on track; shame is when I admit I *am* a mistake. We will later explore this affect in terms of its similarity to pride. With this sense of diminishment or worthlessness, there is, thirdly, an overriding fear of exposure, of being found out to be this terrible person.

The notion of shame, so much discussed in the recovery literature, is one of the most salient and perceptive articulations of what contributes to human misery and misfortune. Shame is the principle driving the maintenance of the facade, the image management that carries the false self along. Shame feeds on secrets, on keeping one's past and parenting realities hidden. Shame nurtures so-called family loyalties by which a person denies reality in the service of clinging to a meager sense of belongingness.

Shame is an all too common and deadly syndrome for clergy because they are especially exposed to public scrutiny. Their shame over addictive and emotional problems is more intense than the general public's. For example, a clergyperson's divorce or alcohol problem is likely to become known to thousands of people in a denomination. Also, certain natural and human feelings are shamed by the expectation of both society and church that clergy should be "glad" and not express anger, hurt, or fear.

The Perspective of the Twelve Steps

The process of healing can also be examined in terms of the famous Twelve Steps of Alcoholics Anonymous. If we look for a moment at that progression, we can recognize that recovery always involves a profound spiritual transformation.

The healing process is begun with Step One, the admission of unmanageability and powerlessness. This is a process of "uncovery," unmasking the false self. It is a de-illusionment, a process of shedding the illusion of power and control.

If, however, the recovering person is to move beyond this moment of "uncovery" toward the eventual new birth of the originally intended "child of God," he or she must undergo a true conversion of mind and heart to the ineffable reality of God.

Steps Two and Three form the true entry-way into a life of recovery. Here one admits that there is a Power higher than either the object of one's addiction or oneself, that this Higher Power can restore one to sanity or wholeness, and that one needs to make a surrender of one's controlling will and willfulness to the care of God as God is understood.

The "surrender" in Step Three is a giving up of all efforts to control or be self-sufficient, a yielding to the mystery of God, an act of unqualified dependence on the Love from which one's life springs.

In Jung's vision, this is the beginning of the second journey; in the vision of John's gospel prologue, it is the beginning of the dynamic of becoming a child of God. We believe that a similar process is available for all who have been wounded in their pasts, regardless of degree.

The Importance of Community

It is important to note the indispensable function of community in enabling and sustaining the individual's movement of recovery. In the community of recovering persons the individual can come to admit the full extent of his or her unmanageable behavior and powerlessness (Step One), come to believe that a Higher Power can restore him or her to sanity (Step Two), and entrust his or her will and life utterly to the care of God (Step Three).

A person who has been emotionally isolated gradually learns to become interdependent with others who understand and care. This draws a person out of the false attitude of attempting to be god of his or her own universe. In becoming part of a true "we," such a person also begins to get an inkling of the ultimate ground of every human "we." Putting it another way, the love and care of the community reveals and makes plausible the love that God is.

The Slow Healing of Shame

In this process, one also comes to a deep appreciation of one's own goodness as affirmed by God. The terrible global shame from which so many clergy suffer is gradually drained away and displaced by humble but healthy self-love before God. For many, this is a long, slow process that only begins during the weeks of treatment.

In the growing certainty of being accepted, forgiven, and cherished, one is able to look more and more objectively at all the false thinking, feeling, and behavior in one's own life (taking a moral inventory humbly, without scrupulosity or self-condemnation) and admit this to God in the presence of another person (Steps Four and Five). This leads to a gradual, day-by-day reshaping of one's way of thinking, feeling, and behaving. In effect, he or she enters upon a life-long process of ongoing recovery (the remaining steps). This includes a commitment to the practice of prayer and meditation (Step Eleven) and culminates in bringing the message to others (Step Twelve).

We have heard many clergy tell us that they were ordained to go out and do the equivalent of Step-Twelve work, that is, to go out and share the Good News of salvation with others. The trouble was, as recovering clergy come to realize, that they had never gone through the first eleven steps (the process of "uncovery," discovery, and recovery) before going out to be ambassadors to others.

The Need for Humility

The opening and surrender to God is basic to the dynamic of recovery, yet this does not come easily to many clergy in treatment. No matter how well trained in theology or how eloquent in speaking of God to others, they find themselves personally empty and hungry, in urgent need of a new discovery of the living God.

The path of recovery for them is a "low road" of suffering, shame, repentance, and becoming "little" (able to learn something new, after being a "God expert" for others for so long). The virtue most needed is humility—resolute honesty in affirming the truth of one's life.

CHAPTER III

Intimacy with Self

"Uncovery," discovery, and recovery can be regarded as stages in the process of attaining intimacy with self. Chapters I and II have been about coming to terms with one's various selves: the false self, the actual self, and the true self. For some, as we have seen, it is also a matter of dealing with the symptomatic self.

From a developmental perspective, we note that some impaired clergy in their twenties and thirties can be so addicted that a false self is obvious; others can be so personality-disordered that the false self is hidden and well managed.

The majority of clergy, of course, are basically healthy in these decades and do not have to deal with the appearance of a symptomatic self. Yet even they must face their incompleteness and the possibility of further growth and challenge. The point is well illustrated by the fact that many actors in their twenties and thirties will refuse to take on the role of King Lear until they are older and more seasoned by life.

Today the pattern of development for clergy is changing in a way that makes for greater complexity. While candidates were once trained and ordained in their twenties, recent trends are toward delayed or second vocations, with training beginning in the thirties. So the midlife crisis/opportunity now tends to appear earlier in the clergy's career. People in the pews tend to expect more seasoned career maturity in clergy facing their fifth decade of life, yet many forty-year-old clergy have only been ordained for a few years and lack pastoral and human experience.

Midlife De-Illusionment

In midlife a process of de-illusionment is required to bring healing to the impaired. To a different degree it is also necessary to bring growth and completeness to the healthy.

Some de-illusionment occurs naturally in midlife and can be called "scheduled" or expected. On a physical level, biological processes and activity levels slow down. On a psycho-social level, children leave home, parents sicken and die, and friends move away. One faces one's own mortality and begins to view time in a different manner, measuring one's span of years not so much from birth but from the perspective of how many years are left. Worldly power and career and financial success and achievements are questioned as to their real significance. Such awards no longer meet one's needs for appreciation and nurturance. Values are clarified and altered. Such changes are normal and appropriate to midlife. Here we must learn to accept our limitations, boundaries, and defects.

Most clergy go through these predictable stresses of midlife without the appearance of disabling or distressing symptoms.

For others, impaired with addictions or other disorders in their twenties and thirties, the de-illusionment in midlife is prompted by the manifestation of crises or symptoms. Depression or anxiety appears, inappropriate sexual behavior is exposed, drunkenness is observed, or one's ministry is terminated due to some alienating behavior such as an explosive temper. These symptoms or crises might be called "unscheduled" or unexpected, not part of the normal range of life predictions.

Yet, whether it is scheduled de-illusionment or an unscheduled crisis, all clergy in midlife will face an opportunity, a chance for healing or growth toward completeness. This opportunity refocuses attention on the appropriate care of self.

Self-Intimacy

How does one take proper care of self, so as to weather these scheduled or unscheduled crises? The appropriate care for self requires the experience of self-intimacy, regardless of how it comes about.

"You've got to take care of yourself." "Get a grip on your life"—
such are frequently the words of advice given to impaired or troubled
clergy by well-meaning friends and lay leaders. Such clergy, though,
have no ears to hear such advice. The words seem to be empty cliches or
they prompt vain and quickly discarded resolutions that make them feel
even more helpless or hopeless.

What does this recommended care of self really mean? Do well-
wishers expect the impaired and troubled to organize their lives around
three moderate meals of the proper food groups? Join health clubs for
regular aerobic exercise and stress reduction? Or sign up for self-
improvement courses at local colleges? Worthy as these activities might
be, those to whom they are recommended either do not hear or follow
through on the advice.

Appreciation of Self

What if a person lacks the basic prerequisites for care of self: ownership
and appreciation of self? If one's affective life is separated from the
cognitive, so that emotional energy is diverted to the service of managing
an image or facade, how can that person have a basic, foundational self-
appreciation? If one is ever looking outside oneself for external sources
of validation and approval, how can one begin to value and trust the self
as a consistent and adequate resource? How can one learn to accept
oneself as one is—limits, defects, and all?

What's more, there is often a paralyzing fear of being exposed as
lacking or defective at the very core. In such cases, the core-belief is
shame, that sense of ontological failure to live up to expectations. This
core-belief undermines and frustrates attempts by self or others to either
encourage or challenge. It invalidates attempts to care for self.

Having laid this groundwork we need to look closely at the issue of
self-intimacy, which involves a thorough knowledge and appreciation of
one's own life, history, and limitations.

Self-intimacy grows and is impacted by the concomitant but often
not simultaneous experiences of intimacy with others and intimacy with
God. Indeed, all three levels of intimacy are intertwined and either
nourish or starve one another. If one arena for intimacy is crippled, the
others are also handicapped.

Self-intimacy is not a given, not congenital; it is achieved only through a life-long process. Families of origin can prepare the soil, model the prerequisites, and nourish the capacity for self-intimacy. Or, as noted earlier, they can deform this capacity.

Self-Intimacy and Identity

The word *intimacy*, of course, is ordinarily used to characterize relationships with others. It may seem odd to apply this word to the self's relationship to itself. But this usage may become more intelligible if we consider for a moment Erikson's developmental stage of "identity," which he posits as a requirement for interpersonal intimacy (Erikson, 1963).

Erikson regards identity as a grounding of the self, a knowledge of who one is—vocationally, sexually, and ideologically. Self-intimacy in our sense includes all this, but is even more: It means knowing oneself emotionally and *appreciating* what one sees. Its antagonist is shame, the despising of self.

Self-Depreciation

A young person leaves home generally with a sense of self-appreciation or self-depreciation. Self-depreciators cannot be intimate with self for they do not have a basic liking for themselves and cannot accept their limitations or forgive their past mistakes. Rather, they brood over these and are painfully aware of their limitations, deficits, and defects. They assume the negative evaluations of past significant others to be true, and they internalize them. Then they reflexively project these onto other people so that they live always in avoidance of a feared rejection by others. They are adept at maintaining secrets, particularly about their pasts and parents.

As described earlier, the healing process for self-depreciators can begin when the separation of head and heart begins to be overcome. This occurs with the felt experience of pain—pain in the form of grief, hurt, sadness, fear, or anger as focused and aimed at the ones who originally caused the pain.

Healing occurs as one is able to access and express this pain. This process is healing because it engenders a sense of safety and trust for one's own experience as reliable, including one's feelings. When this process begins, self-depreciators also realize how much they are still shaming their feelings, a deadly habit they learned from their own significantly shaming others.

The Spiritual Dimension of Self-Intimacy

Ultimately, the attaining of self-intimacy is a spiritual quest. The needed appreciation of the self cannot be contingent upon one's heritage, one's productive capacities, or one's achievements. Genuine self-esteem and self-appreciation can only be *received* as ultimately God-given. As Gerald May has written, the heart must be awakened to its own worth and appreciation (G. May, 1991).

This is where secular philosophies and theories of counseling must make a spiritual leap of humanistic if not quasi-religious faith. They must rely on foundational presuppositions or givens, such as human-kind's basic goodness, as obvious or self-evident.

We, however, turn at this point to the theological notion of "what God intended" as revealed in the Word. This is the mystery of each human person as "child of God"—created as lovable and cherishable, deserving of nurturance and care.

To see oneself through the eyes of God, as revealed in Scripture and mediated through a caring community, is to believe oneself worthy of appreciation. This sense of selfworth is intrinsic, sans contingency or achievement.

This truth of the individual's worth in God's eyes, quite prior to any achievement, is conveyed in infant baptism as practiced by most churches. The infant is clearly incapable of external achievement or success. The grace of God is given in baptism as a pure gift, undeserved and undeservable. Conferring this on infants brings home this basic spiritual truth: We are intrinsically and spiritually lovable.

Two Views of Human Development

To illustrate the significance of the crisis/opportunity of self-intimacy in
the emotional breakdown of midlife, we can look at the two parabolas in
Diagram 1. Our ordinary view of life as an upward parabola sees an
ascent in earlier years, followed by a decline or descent in the later ones.
The apex is midlife, after which the lifeline is seen as moving downhill.
This is a view bolstered by biological and psycho-social realities: After
forty we experience a bodily decline and a loss of friends, relatives, and
children. The shrinkage of one's biological and social worlds often
culminates in an old-age preoccupation with one's physical levels of
functioning. For some elderly, their bodies become their world.

We propose to turn this parabola upside down to depict the course of
spiritual growth and progress. Now the nadir comes in midlife, where
one bottoms out from the previous overreliance on self alone for success
and achievement, which are measured externally by worldly standards.
This downward portion of the spiritual journey corresponds with Jung's
"the morning of life" with less spiritual awareness and more materialistic
activity and preoccupation. We are familiar with the deceptive claims
that such achievements are done for the glory of God or as a sign of
God's favor.

The spiritual lifeline, then, at midlife takes off upward and opens up
new possibilities not available before. The "law of the afternoon," in
Jung's phrase, is developmentally more open and available to the spiritual growth potential of the second journey.

This second parabola brings hope to those who have hit a particular
bottom in their midlife courses, whether it be substance abuse, depression, alienation, perpetration of abuse, or some other crisis. The false
self (or at least, the incompleteness) of the earlier decades is brought,
through symptoms or crisis, to the low point of the actual self, and then
shown the opportunity of a journey upward toward the true self, the
originally intended "child of God."

Various Possibilities of Self-Orientation

The self's intimate relationship to itself can be illustrated in another
diagram that will be continually augmented as we discuss issues relative

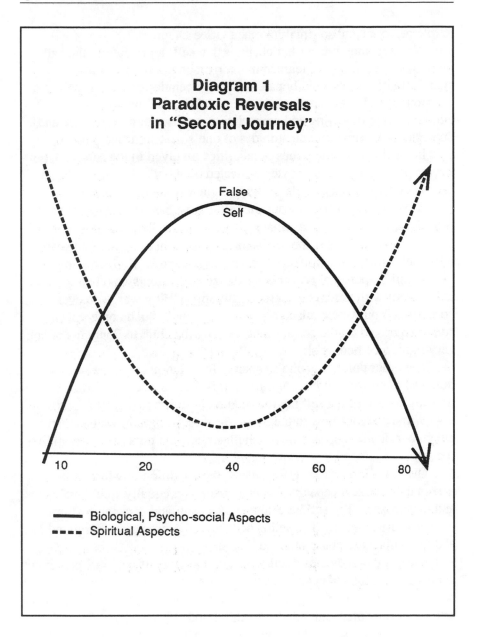

**Diagram 1
Paradoxic Reversals
in "Second Journey"**

False
Self

10   20   40   60   80

——— Biological, Psycho-social Aspects
- - - - Spiritual Aspects

to interpersonal and spiritual intimacy. (See Diagram 2.)

We have shown in earlier chapters that self-appreciation, the hall-mark of self-intimacy, is learned in interpersonal relationships with significant others, especially parents. One's relationship to oneself is a consequence of one's past development. This relationship to self can be either intimate (knowing and appreciative) or disordered (unaware and depreciative), mirroring the attitudes of one's past significant others.

In the diagram, the issues or polarities involved in the self's relationship to itself are personal power, indicated on the y axis, and one's capacity or openness for relationships, indicated on the x axis.

Personal power here means the self's most basic sense of entitlement for its very existence, what Rollo May has called "the power to be" (R. May, 1972). This is the self's grasp of its right to be here, to share life in this world. It is foundational to any sense of self-affirmation.

A child's personal power is vandalized by parents who batter the child's soul with verbal contempt of this sort: "Why were you ever born?" or "You were a mistake—or an accident." Such contempt becomes engraved on the child's soul, causing the child to doubt his or her very right to be here at all.

The other polarity is one's capacity for relationships, the sense or felt need to be with another or others. It is akin to a sense of trust, but here it is a trust of the self not to fragment in the company of others.

With reference now to the two axes of this diagram, we can distinguish four quadrants, each of which illustrates one possible orientation of the self.

Quadrant I indicates self-intimacy, the condition in which both personal power and capacity for relationship are equally well developed and maximized. The self here appreciates itself and is capable of relationship outside itself. The self is neither self-depreciatory nor grandiose and has no need to abuse others or itself.

Quadrant II indicates a self with a high degree of personal power but a diminished sense of need and capacity for intimacy with others. Such a self is grandiose or self-aggrandizing. It may be narcissistic or extremely self-focused or preoccupied, due to childhood deprivations. This self feels okay about its right to be here but is capable of infringing on others' rights and boundaries.

Quadrant III indicates both the self's hatred of self and a diminished capacity for relationship. Persons in this quadrant minimize their power

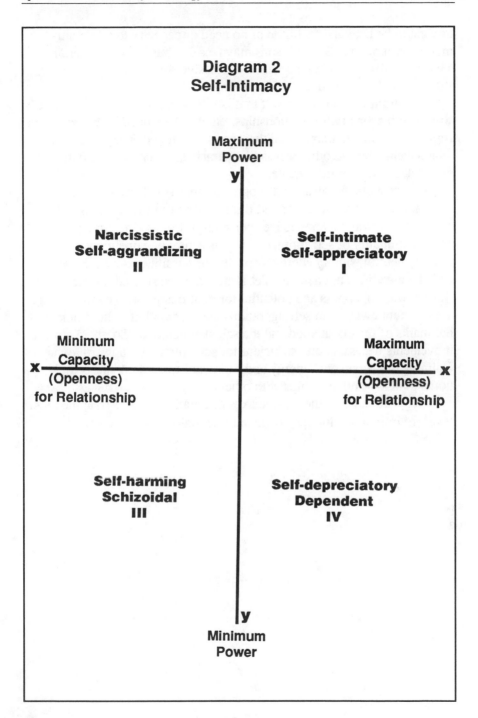

Diagram 2
Self-Intimacy

Maximum
Power
y

Narcissistic
Self-aggrandizing
II

Self-intimate
Self-appreciatory
I

Minimum
Capacity
(Openness)
for Relationship
x

Maximum
Capacity
(Openness)
for Relationship
x

Self-harming
Schizoidal
III

Self-depreciatory
Dependent
IV

y
Minimum
Power

or right to be here and feel little or no need or capacity to relate intimately with others. Such persons may be self-abusive or self-harming.
They may also be schizoidal with a depressive self-depreciation. They
are profoundly shamed and self-shaming.

Quadrant IV indicates a self that is self-depreciatory but quite needy
with a high capacity for relationships. Such selves have minimized their
right to be here and maximized their need for others. They cling or
attach themselves to other selves like parasites. Such persons may be
called dependent or inadequate.

The movement toward self-appreciation, the hallmark of self-
intimacy, is toward the upper and right quadrant of the diagram. The
movement upward acknowledges personal power as a necessary but not
sufficient quality of self-intimacy. In this sense, personal power is
morally neutral, simply energy, capacity, or possibility. This power must
be acknowledged, not denied. Yet it must also be steered toward the
right, toward openness and potential for relationship with others. This is
a movement away from self-aggrandizement or exploitation of others—
hallmarks of the dissatisfied and the self-depreciative. So, there are two
movements necessary and sufficient for self-intimacy: upward toward
claiming one's personal energy and rightward toward openness for
nonexploitative relationships with others.

We will be using these same axes or polarities to illustrate the other
levels of intimacy—interpersonal and spiritual—in subsequent chapters.

CHAPTER IV

Interpersonal Intimacy

In everyday usage, the word *intimacy* most often refers to interpersonal relationships. The word normally characterizes a relationship between two people and is often confused with something sexual. Short of that use, its meaning remains elusive and difficult to articulate.

The Meaning of Intimacy

Harry Stack Sullivan defines it as a relationship between two people that encourages the building up of self-worth and is characterized by a kind of collaboration in which one adjusts expectations to the needs of the other (Sullivan, 1953).

Eric Berne calls it a candid and honest emotional exchange (Berne, 1964). He maintains that there are only three possible human transactions: pastimes, games, or intimacy. Pastimes are routine, superficial remarks, "How are you?" Games are the many dishonest manipulations and hidden agendas among people. The only emotionally honest and candid interchanges are called intimacy.

Etymologically, the word itself comes from the Latin word *intus*, meaning "inside"; its comparative is *interior*, meaning "more inside"; the superlative is *intimus*, meaning the "most inside." The Latin word *intimus*, therefore, can also mean "best friend." The whole series denotes depth and interiority, a sharing of one's insides with another. As we will discuss later, using Sullivan's phrases, this intimacy has little or nothing to do with approximating genitals one to another's.

In Sullivan's schema, intimacy is the second to develop of the three integrating forces of personality. The first is self-worth, that absence of shame we have discussed. The third is genital sexuality, which we will discuss later in this chapter.

Intimacy in its nascent form first appears as a need in pre- or early-adolescence with the appearance of a same-sex best friend or chum, a confidant. This first best-friend experience contains elements of sharing secrets, a nonjudgmental acceptance, and an answer to the emerging problem of loneliness. Significantly, in this schema, this need is prior developmentally to genital sexuality and separable from it. Intimacy is primarily an attitude; sex is an act.

Alternatives to Intimacy

There are many barriers as well as counterfeits to interpersonal intimacy. In short, we can say that disorders, abuse, addictions, and compulsions are what we do instead of intimacy. The alcoholic, for example, has a love-affair with a chemical—a love-affair the alcoholic thinks he or she can control and use reliably to alter mood and anesthetize pain.

The common counterfeits and barriers to intimacy may be graphed on the same axes previously used to explicate self-intimacy. (See Diagram 3.) The polarities are power and relationship. We again use the y axis for the sense of power and the x axis for the importance of relationships.

Power is the sense of affirmation and assertiveness one possesses. We mean personal or personality power primarily. But it is important to note that clergy have an additional capacity for power that comes from their role and status in society as objects of fiduciary trust and respect, regardless of their own awareness of or feel for such power. Here, relationship means the actual state of one's interpersonal world or interest in that world.

When we combine the two axes and graph four quadrants, we arrive at some important variables and relationships that help explicate the common barriers and counterfeits to interpersonal intimacy.

We begin with the counterfeits of Quadrant II. Here we graph people who are high on power and low on relationship. Their personal power is better developed than their relationship capacity.

Clergy who assume the hero role fit here; they fix others as their way of exerting power over others. Often hidden here is a controlling

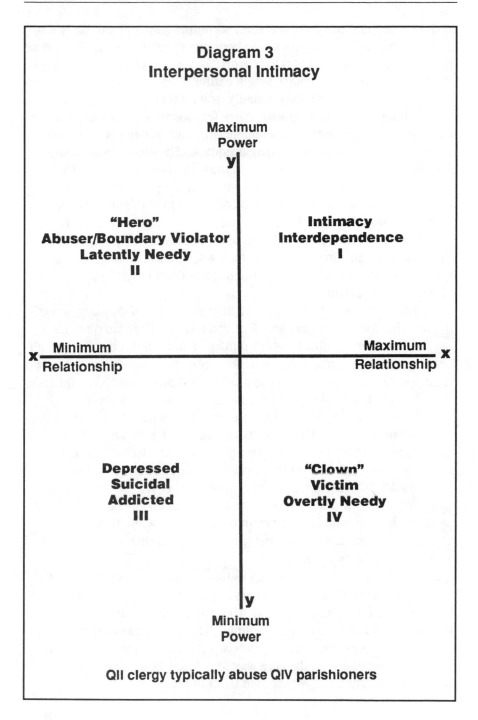

Diagram 3
Interpersonal Intimacy

Maximum Power
y

"Hero"
Abuser/Boundary Violator
Latently Needy
II

Intimacy
Interdependence
I

x Minimum Relationship

Maximum Relationship x

Depressed
Suicidal
Addicted
III

"Clown"
Victim
Overtly Needy
IV

y
Minimum Power

QII clergy typically abuse QIV parishioners

and dominating type of manipulation accompanied by grandiose fanta-
sies of power adequate to fix anybody or any problem. Such clergy need
to be right and to have others to control, fix up, and correct or instruct.
We have discussed this role at length earlier.

Clergy who abuse others sexually or who transgress sexual or
physical boundaries fit here also. They fear losing their power, which
signifies their autonomy. They fear getting involved in peer relationships in which they would be seen as equals. They are afraid of being
"swallowed up" by others who match them in power or status. They
avoid such threatening relationships. Instead, they cross boundaries and
abuse those weaker or with less role and status than themselves; they
typically abuse their parishioners or those who come to them for help.

They are often deluded enough to think they are helping their victims, being magnanimous and generous with their time and energy. The
illusion of altruistic generosity is often maintained by elaborate systems
of denial justification.

These Quadrant II clergy believe they are agents of intimacy, model-
ing such behavior for needy and deprived others. They are often igno-
rant of their own neediness, which remains latent until it breaks through
boundaries when connected with another obviously needy per-son. Two
needy people of unequal power in a close relationship often masquerade
intimacy and nearly always court emotional disaster and abuse.

We turn now to their obverse, those in Quadrant IV. These are the
placaters or clowns we have already discussed. These are high on relationships and low on power. They become chameleons, bending and
measuring their behavior in reaction to the perceived approval of others.
For the sake of maintaining a relationship at all costs, they subordinate
and minimize self. This is the *locus classicus* of codependency. Many
clergy fit here in terms of their church leadership, while they fit in
Quadrant II when relating to their spouses and families. They are wimps
at work and tyrants at home.

Another group of increasingly outspoken people also fit here—the
victims of clergy abuse and boundary violations. They are often overtly
needy but basically healthy people who come to the pastor and church in
times of situational distress and trouble. They can also be more dis-
turbed individuals, past victims of abuse who come to the pastor in a
pathetically sexual way, the only way they knew how to get approval
from a significant other who abused them in their past.

Far too often, Quadrant II clergy will continue to abuse and revictimize such tragic people. Such clergy maintain the illusion of a healing touch or intimacy that the victim needs to bolster a battered self-esteem. We have encountered many clergy who have maintained that they received no pleasure in sex with such victims, that they were only giving and not receiving.

If we examine Quadrant III we see the convergence of those who are low on power and low on relationship. For them nothing counts but the termination of their pain and discomfort. They themselves don't count; relationships don't count; nothing matters at all. Such people lose interest both in relationships and in their own goals and needs. They tend to isolate themselves and disengage from life. They block awareness of needs and painful feelings with substance abuse or other addictions to food or sex.

These are the depressed, the despairing, and the addicted who find fake intimacy in their objects of addictiveness. Their feelings are numbed by their depressions, compulsions, and addictions. This is true especially for compulsive sexual behaviors, where orgasms momentarily numb the pain through the experience of ecstasy. At times, clergy fall into this quadrant, either exclusively or intermittently after experiencing the failures of intimacy in Quadrants II and IV. They may ultimately choose to numb or permanently anesthetize their pain by suicide.

Finally, we come to Quadrant I, the area for interpersonal intimacy. Here we locate those who are high both in personal power and in capacity for relationship. They maximize their capacity and need for relationship, while they maximize their capacity and need to maintain their own personal power.

They are aware of and respect emotional, physical, and sexual boundaries and have no need to cross over and violate another's boundaries to bolster their own low power or low self-esteem. Avoiding the codependency of Quadrant IV and the counter-dependency (the paradoxical need to be needed, which is just as codependent as the need to be in need) of Quadrant II, those capable of genuine intimacy practice interdependency, a give-and-take between peers of equal power.

Clergy Sexual Abuse

The schema we have been following allows us to understand better the matter of clergy sexual abuse, a topic of growing concern and exposure. There is a special, morbid relationship between Quadrant II clergy and Quadrant IV victims. They seem to gravitate toward one another and create the potential for abuse and harm if the cleric is not aware of self, not self-intimate, not aware of interpersonal dynamics in relationships.

The cleric is in the position of power. By definition of the word *affair*, no cleric can have one with a parishioner; the boundary violation of such a sexual relationship goes beyond any marital or family system connoted by the word *affair*. It violates the pastoral relationship, a professional boundary. Increasingly, state legislatures are making such a boundary violation a serious criminal offense.

One difficulty is that clergy generally do not *feel* powerful; in fact, they feel powerless. They tend to view power in worldly terms, with materialistic conceptions of success. Clergy are not wealthy, do not hold public offices, do not even claim or want to be powerful. In fact, the clergy's status is falling. Once they were high-status and low-paid; now they are more low-status and low-paid.

On the other hand, these worldly standards are in contrast to the symbolic and personal power that comes with the role. Clergy wear distinctive clothes, wear symbolic and ritualized vestments while presiding up front in worship, and deliver sermons, one-way communications that are neither challenged nor questioned. While the role of the church and its clergy may have declined in society, the pastor still has considerable power and a fiduciary responsibility in the parish or neighborhood community.

Dynamically, when a narcissistic cleric meets an obviously needy and distressed parishioner who comes for help, the probability for abuse is high. Clergy often identify and come to terms with their narcissism only after such violations of boundaries or abuses occur. When, in hindsight, they realize that their own latent neediness broke through their usual restraint and control and violated another person, only then can they accept such a diagnosis. We believe narcissism is involved whenever one's needs become so urgent and demanding as to cross over sacred boundaries of other persons.

Sexuality

Intimacy is commonly confused with sexuality. The question, "Were you intimate?" is interchangeable with "Did you have sex?" Sexuality, however, may be an integrated part of intimacy or may have a separate life of its own. As stated earlier, intimacy is an attitude, a spiritual quality; sex is an act. The sexual act may mean many things other than intimacy: violence, commercial transaction, or playtime *a la* the *Playboy* philosophy.

We find that clergy who manifest sexual misconduct or transgress boundaries generally are impoverished as far as intimacy with self, others, and God is concerned. Part of the problem is ecclesiogenic (having its origin from the church), especially in religious traditions and formations that have severely shamed human sexuality.

Often in their attempts to prevent the acts of sex from occurring, such traditions have also, as an unfortunate side-effect, prevented the growth of intimacy. For example, many Roman Catholic clergy and religious now in midlife were prohibited in their earlier, significantly formative years from cultivating so-called "particular friendships," in effect stifling any possibility of interpersonal intimacy. There appears to have been a parallel hypervigilance in some Protestant seminaries as well.

Five Stances Toward Sexuality

There are four problematic stances that one can adopt toward one's sexuality, each of which can also be fostered by religious tradition and formation. There is a fifth stance, which we will call and depict as "integrative," that is the only one compatible with intimacy.

The first of the possible stances toward sexuality is *repression*. This is to pretend that one is not sexual at all. It is to try to live an asexual life because of the deep anxiety and shame triggered by sexual impulses. Sullivan describes a "primary genital phobia," a condition wherein sexual thoughts, feelings, and impulses are almost immediately and reflexively ignored and denied (Sullivan, 1953).

We have met many clergy who in midlife are unsure of their basic sexual orientation because whenever they had a sexual impulse they so shut it off that they ceased to be aware of sexuality at all. Some religious traditions with a dualistic or puritanical philosophy have engendered and fostered such a stance. Sexual impulses are regarded as proximate occasions of sin and dangerous to one's salvation. Yet sexuality is a core human experience and cannot be ignored or repressed without some serious emotional repercussion. Typically, in a midlife crisis/opportunity the repressed cleric's sexuality will explode in some inappropriate and arrested manifestation, such as sexual contact with a minor.

A second stance, similar to the first but with more active use of will power, is *suppression.* Here a person actually and consciously struggles against sexual impulses. This person remains vigilant, guarded, and in active combat, with will power as major armament against the intrusion and invasion of sexual imagination. Note the imagery of warfare and battle. We hear of "white knuckling" and cold showers as ways to arrest, stifle, and terminate sexual impulses that have become threatening to one's emotional and spiritual well-being.

This mechanism was once presented as a major tool against masturbation, which was regarded as seriously sinful. The fallacy was twofold here. First, masturbation was not seen as a probable symptom of loneliness and intimacy-deprivation, especially when compulsive. Instead, it was simply moralized as sinful and condemned along with the person who engaged in it. Sullivan wisely states that one cannot meet one's need for intimacy all by oneself, that the isolation of masturbation cannot quench the desire for intimacy that is obviously lacking in the compulsive use of masturbation. On a humorous note, he goes on to say that what makes masturbation an emotional problem is that it can "keep one from meeting interesting people" (Sullivan, 1953).

The second fallacy has to do with human attention. By focusing attention on not masturbating, one is focusing on the act and will eventually give in. One becomes preoccupied and eventually obsessed with the behavior. Will power alone as a tool against such behavior fails and leaves one with more shame as morally weak and a failure. Suppression leads to preoccupation which leads to obsession, which eventually leads to gratification.

The third possibility, then, is *gratification*—the stance of our age, the sexual revolution, though recently reevaluated in light of AIDS. Such a stance is also dualistic; Rollo May terms it "the new Puritanism" (R. May, 1969). It uses the body as a pleasure machine, to be turned off and on, detached from relationship and intimacy. It is dualistic since it, too, like repression, splits mind from body. Actually, such a stance risks trivializing sexuality and debasing its erotic power and significance, its deep longing for fulfillment. Gratification can become compulsive-addictive, and sexuality so gratified can become empty and meaningless repetition. This addictiveness can characterize the stance of clergy who have established patterns of sexual misconduct.

The fourth stance is favored by Freudians: *sublimation*. This is a channeling of sexual energy—libido—toward artistic and creative pursuits. To view libido as the life force and to want to canalize it in directions of creativity is an offshoot of psychoanalytic theory, which reduces the life of the spirit to the biological. According to such theory, we are motivated and pushed, as it were, from within by sexual drives.

What is missing in this theory is a properly spiritual perspective that could view us as not only pushed by drives, but also "pulled" by a personal God toward a relationship of intimacy. In such a view, our sexual desires would find their meaning in our being called and invited to a dimension of intimacy, a level beyond the biophysical order.

Last, there is the stance toward sexuality that we will call *integration*. This is a process of making ever more sense of one's total experience of mind, body, and spirit. It is incarnational in the sense that spirituality in our tradition is bound up with the enfleshment of God in Christ. Integration does not ignore (repress), fight against (suppress), put parentheses around (sublimate), or simply give in to (gratify) sexual thoughts, feelings, and impulses. Rather, integration honestly faces and addresses sexuality in the total context of intimacy with self, others, and God.

The model we present uses Sullivanian categories to open up to the primacy of interpersonal intimacy but expands this integrating experience to include intimacy with self and with God.

Sullivan's developmental view is visualized in Diagram 4, which depicts three building blocks, one resting upon another. These correspond to the developmental progression from childhood through preadolescence and adolescence, in Sullivanian theory.

The bottom block, the foundational support, is the experience of self-esteem, the absence of crippling and toxic shame—which is highly influenced by parenting, as described earlier.

If this foundation is in place, the next block—of intimacy—can be safely added. Without this firm foundation of self-esteem, one cannot

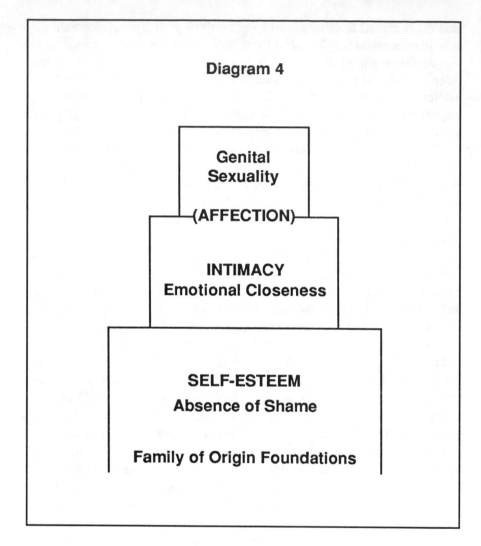

Diagram 4

Genital
Sexuality

(AFFECTION)

INTIMACY
Emotional Closeness

SELF-ESTEEM
Absence of Shame

Family of Origin Foundations

safely risk an emotional closeness with another without fear of losing a fragile autonomy or identity. With the foundation, one can safely risk and develop such closeness.

The top block in the diagram represents genital sexuality. When established on these two supporting blocks, it is integrated, connected, and unlikely to develop a life all its own or to become compulsive/ addictive.

When there is sufficient self-esteem and a healthy intimacy with self, others, and God, sexuality becomes less a driven compulsion or solution for loneliness and more a free choice that is appropriate to one's personal lifestyle choice.

On the other hand, what happens when a shame-filled pastor with low self-esteem and no intimate friends encounters a delayed genital sexuality for the first time as a powerful and driving force? In our clinical experience, we have too often seen that the drive is gratified, often in inappropriate ways. When self-esteem is shamed, when sexuality is shamed, when intimacy and friendship are shamed, we can always expect trouble.

Sexual Integration for Clergy

Of course ordination across the traditions does not require lifestyle uniformity. We choose to divide clergy into three categories: Married clergy, as permitted in the Protestant, Anglican, and Orthodox traditions; celibate or vowed clergy and/or religious, as mandated in Roman Catholicism and an option in Orthodoxy and Anglicanism; and single clergy as found in Protestant and Anglican churches.

It is our premise that, regardless of clerical lifestyle, the general picture conveyed by the building-blocks diagram still holds: The necessity of self-esteem and intimacy as foundational is valid for all. Whether or not genital sexuality can be integrated depends on the choice of lifestyle. Sexual gratification, of course, can occur across all these styles, but the matter at hand is whether *integration* can occur. Let us review these lifestyles and their implications for the integration of genital sexuality.

Married clergy: Married clergy have a structural ideal for integration;

integration of one's self-esteem, interpersonal intimacy, and genital sexuality can be focused in one relationship. This one relationship is exclusive, permanent, and committed. It has the time and place for genitality and is open to a history.

Celibate clergy: Celibate and vowed clergy and religious have a different commitment and integrating task. They have a relationship to their community, which is framed as exclusive, permanent, and committed. The community and/or the Church becomes the focus. While one's needs for self-esteem and intimacy with others can be met and concretized in these wider relationships, there is no optional integrating place for genitality. The commitment is not to one special other but to the community, a wider diffusion of interpersonal energy.

Unfortunately, many (diocesan) celibate clergy today are forced to live alone, without a household community, because of the scarcity of vocations. Even members of religious orders increasingly find themselves living without the support of a large community, as was formerly the norm.

Single clergy: Those clergy who are single as a vocational choice, that is, those who freely intend not to marry, have a different task of integration. They are committed to the Church, which becomes the focus of their energy. Unlike the vowed, they usually lack the opportunity to live in a community household, and live alone much like celibate clergy. The importance of intimacy with self, others, and God becomes even more pronounced in this lifestyle choice.

Single clergy are the most misunderstood of these groups. Indeed, just as in Roman Catholicism celibacy is a required condition for ordination, so in Protestantism is marriage practically mandatory for advancement and avoidance of homophobic prejudice.

Chastity

Chastity is the unifying virtue that cuts across the differences in lifestyle. It is an ideal for all, not just a specialized vow for religious communities. It means fidelity, single-mindedness, a lack of duplicity. These qualities are needed in married, celibate-vowed, and single lifestyles.

Fidelity, according to Erikson, is the virtue or strength necessary for adulthood (Erikson, 1963). This means the ability to make and keep one's commitments, as freely made. To make a commitment is the sign of maturity. A commitment is also the enhancer of intimacy, as is permanence and a history.

All clergy in whatever lifestyles make commitments, try to be faithful to them, and fail at them as well as manage to succeed in keeping them. Commitment, for our limited humanity in this life, is by definition always a matter of being half-sure and whole-hearted. We never know nor can we guarantee the future.

Commitments fail, but this does not mean that they should never be made. Consider the alternatives. One can be half-sure and half-hearted. This is to demand guarantees before being willing to commit. Those who play at marriage by living together, for instance, hedge their bets and remain half-hearted. They risk remaining faint-hearted, lacking the whole-heartedness of commitment, the ability to give with full generosity.

Or, one can be wholly sure and whole-hearted, a fanatic without any doubts or fear or struggle. Some fundamentalist clergy fall into this category. They, too, fear making a commitment and the risks involved, and prefer to believe there are no risks at all, since all outcomes are predictable and guaranteed.

We argue, therefore, that commitment is necessary for the framework of integrating genitality, even though we are aware of the many failures and the intrinsic risks. Indeed, this whole matter of sexual integration proceeds by a kind of trial-and-error learning, where every person remains his or her own pioneer, makes mistakes, one hopes becomes the wiser for them, and tries again. Chastity—fidelity—is an ideal that is bound up with the necessary tentativeness and risk taking of adulthood which itself depends on self-esteem and intimacy proficiencies.

Summary

Integration is an ideal and a goal, as well as a process. It is learned by making mistakes. We strive to integrate our human sexuality into meaningful contexts of intimacy in such ways as not to damage our self-esteem.

All need intimacy for emotional and spiritual survival. Genital sexuality is not required for the survival of an individual; it is necessary for the species' survival.

Different expressions and traditions of clerical, ordained lifestyles, despite their divergent attitudes toward genital sexuality, all have something much more fundamental in common. This is the universal human need for intimacy. If we could get the focus away from isolated sexuality and focus instead on the ways and means of meeting our more basic need for intimacy, then we believe the ordained ministry and the whole Body of Christ would be better served.

CHAPTER V

Intimacy with God

As we have seen in the preceding chapter, interpersonal intimacy involves the highest possible degrees of both personal "power" and relationship to others. True interpersonal intimacy does not require that one partner be dependent on or submissive to the other. The relationship of intimacy is one of full mutuality in which the uniqueness and goodness of each party is respected, appreciated, and affirmed.

What are we to say, then, of intimacy with God? This cannot, in the same sense, be a relationship of equals. Yet there is a parallel. The paradox of the divine-human relationship is this: The more closely related the human creature is to God (always involving utter dependence and unqualified "surrender"), the more perfectly individuated and fulfilled the person is (the more personal "power" he or she experiences).

Intimacy with God and Its Counterfeits

It is possible to construct a diagram of four quadrants, parallel to the earlier diagrams, illustrating intimacy with self and intimacy with others. (See Diagram 5.) Once again, the two axes represent power and relationship (to God).

Quadrant I represents the fulfillment of the divinely intended human creature—perfectly individuated and possessing a maximum of personal power, while at the same time related to God in the most intimate possible way. To speak in explicitly Christian theological terms, this relationship to God is not merely as creature, but as redeemed and beloved and caught up (in the Son) into God's own interpersonal life (the mystery of the Trinity). This blessed outcome of a human being's story may also be

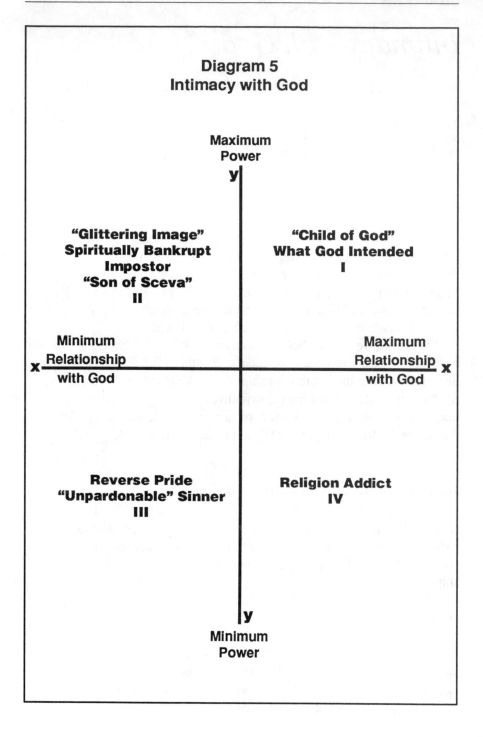

Diagram 5
Intimacy with God

Maximum
Power
y

"Glittering Image"   "Child of God"
Spiritually Bankrupt   What God Intended
Impostor   I
"Son of Sceva"
II

Minimum   Maximum
x Relationship   Relationship x
with God   with God

Reverse Pride   Religion Addict
"Unpardonable" Sinner   IV
III

y
Minimum
Power

characterized as becoming finally "child of God" in the Johannine sense as explained in Chapter I.

While this must be regarded as perfectly achieved only at the consummation of all things, it is possible to recognize the beginnings of it in various human stories. Moreover, it must be taken as the ideal of spiritual health and well-being, toward which each person is invited and drawn.

In contrast to this is the spiritual condition indicated by Quadrant II. Here there is a maximum of personal power (or rather the maximum *semblance* of power), but a minimum of real relationship with God. Such a person is really spiritually bankrupt, though perhaps appearing to others as very impressive. One thinks again of the title of Susan Howatch's first novel about the clergy, *Glittering Images*. Such a person is a kind of impostor, trying to seem spiritual while lacking the reality.

One could see this spiritual state illustrated in a story from the Acts of the Apostles (Acts 19:13-17). In this incident, some itinerant Jewish exorcists (the seven sons of a Jewish high priest named Sceva) attempt to drive out evil spirits by calling on the name of "the Jesus whom Paul proclaims."

This indirect way of invoking Christ indicates that they themselves did not know him or relate to him as Lord. They take on the guise of spiritual authority in Jesus' name but without being in personal relationship to God as revealed in Jesus.

The outcome is disastrous for them. The evil spirit they were trying to exorcise says to them: "Jesus I know, and Paul I know; but who are you?" The possessed man then attacks them violently so that "they fled out of the house naked and wounded."

In Quadrant III of the diagram we see the spiritual condition of a person who is likewise minimally related to God, but who is the opposite of the preceding type. This person has a minimal awareness of any personal goodness or power.

People in this quadrant have a keen sense of how utterly wretched and unworthy they are. In fact, they refuse all invitations to receive God's mercy and love (to enter into relationship) on the grounds that they are unpardonable sinners.

In fact, there is a strange kind of "reverse pride" in such a person's stance. While conceding that all others may benefit from God's pardon freely given, such a one is convinced that he or she is irredeemably evil and lost, beyond the imagining of anyone who tries to say otherwise. In this way, this person is able to claim a kind of absolute importance, albeit in a negative way. It is really a form of pride.

Finally, Quadrant IV illustrates another kind of false spiritual stance. This represents a person who, like the previous type, has a minimal sense of self-worth, but who clings to God through religiosity in a compulsive way, *seeming* to be maximally related to God.

One could say that such a person is "addicted" to religion in the sense of adhering with fanatical tenacity to various beliefs and practices as a way of achieving self-worth. But all this religiosity is actually a substitute for that genuine intimacy with God that liberates from self-contempt and all anxiety.

In view of this analysis, the ideal of intimacy with God is clearly designated in contrast to its various counterfeits. But how are we to understand its relevance and possibility for the personal spiritual lives of clergy?

Lack of Intimacy with God in Clergy

As we have seen in an earlier chapter, it is possible for a clergyperson to be alienated from self while ministering devotedly to the needs of others. That is, a cleric can live without sufficient awareness of or respect for the true feelings and needs of the self.

Parallel to this alienation from self very often is a lack of real *personal* relationship to God. The alienation from God is concealed by the cleric's immersion in "the things of God"—teaching, preaching, visiting the sick, praying with others, presiding at liturgy. While sincere, this kind of activity can coexist with an almost complete absence of private, personal presence to God.

Ordained ministers can live for years on the level of the "objective," church-mediated faith (what "we" believe), without reflecting much on their personal history with God, without any heartfelt personal love-involvement with God.

This kind of "existential distance" from God, as already indicated, is usually linked with an alienation from one's own deep personal center. People like this live "on the surface," much of the time simply maintaining a false self that is pleasing and impressive to others.

Also typical for this pattern of life and ministry is a notable split between head and heart. A person in this condition may be well educated in theology and quite eloquent in teaching correct doctrine. His or her preaching and counseling, however, is likely to be without much power to touch the hearts of others.

What is missing in such a life is a deeply lived *love* relationship to the One about whom this person speaks. This is what we are trying to name in speaking of intimacy with God.

The Need for Intimacy with God

The need for this is present in every human being and especially in those who have never known the joy of being loved and affirmed for their own sake. In fact, many clergy have come from families of origin where their need to be appreciated and affirmed as their own unique selves was never met.

Against that background we need to view the familiar pattern among clergy of compulsive overwork and a "driven" way of ministering to the needs of others. They are trying to win the unqualified admiration and love of others by being almost superhumanly "wonderful" in their ministerial role—to fill the aching void within themselves.

We need to recognize the absolute primacy of the love-relationship in everyone's life, including clergy. Each person needs somewhere along the way to discover that he or she is loved, affirmed, appreciated, and cherished prior to all performance.

The discovery that one is loved by God must eventually take priority over all other ways of relating to God. The unqualified love of God for the human creature, redeemed in Christ, is prior to the human admission of guilt and seeking of forgiveness. It is prior to any effort at undertaking works in God's service. It is prior to any proclamation of the Good News to others.

Until one discovers this primal truth, human life will be distorted and driven. In fact, all else should follow from the deep knowledge that one is loved. Without that knowledge, all else is likely to be efforts at self-validation, efforts to ward off shame and condemnation—in short, a lifestyle (especially for clergy) of drivenness.

The Way Toward Intimacy with God

But how is the ordained minister of the Good News to make the personal discovery, firsthand, of his or her own love-relationship with God? So often such a person is busy sincerely assuring *others* that they can benefit from this love-relationship, but this person surprisingly does not really believe (in a deep-down, emotional way) that it applies personally to the preacher.

The discovery of being personally loved and accepted by God comes to many people only through the experience of first being "brought low," that is, failing in some notable way, being "found out" as weak, imperfect, not "having it all together." This is the case, of course, with most of the men and women we have learned from at Saint Barnabas.

In effect, it seems that the realization of just how *poor* one actually is prepares the way to receiving God's unconditional acceptance. One might think of Jesus' saying, "How hard it is for those who have wealth to enter the kingdom of God!" (Luke 18:24) as well as the first of the Beatitudes, "Blessed are the poor in spirit, for theirs is the kingdom of heaven" (Matt. 5:3).

The recognition of one's utter spiritual poverty is often the entry-way into a new level of relationship with the God whom one has believed in and preached about. For this reason, clergy who come for treatment of major disorders in their lives have an opportunity for profound spiritual renewal. Indeed, they cannot find healing without such a renewal.

The Spiritual Dynamic of the Twelve Steps

Much can be learned, in this respect, by looking closely at the spiritual dynamic of the Twelve Steps of Alcoholics Anonymous. Though not explicitly Christian, this program for recovery is profoundly spiritual.

Those who come to A.A. or a similar group are drawn into a momentous spiritual conversion, a drastic change of outlook on reality and their own place within it. They are confronted early on with the most radical issue of all—whether or not to really believe in God.

This issue should not be trivialized. The option to believe in God must never be taken for granted as self-evident or obvious—even for clergy. On the contrary, it is really the decisive choice from which all else follows.

The addicted person, of course, does not come to this issue in a theoretical way but, rather, out of the abject misery of being enslaved to a substance and/or behavior. Hence, the Twelve Steps begin with the honest admission of the utter chaos and unmanageability of the addict's life (Step One).

From the accounts in the "Big Book" of A.A. it seems clear that the decisive move into recovery occurs when the addicted person acknowledges in a real, heartfelt way the unimaginable reality that the word "God" tries to name (Alcoholics Anonymous, 3rd ed., 1976).

Step Two speaks of "coming to believe" that a Power greater than ourselves could restore us to sanity. That moment of "coming to believe" is not a matter of resolving an intellectual doubt. For the addict, it is a choice between despair and hope in the face of enslavement to addiction. This choice to believe in God arises out of desperate need—the need for a Savior.

For clergy, this may mean letting go of shallow, narrow, or misleading notions of God and admitting that God is infinitely great. But this is actually very difficult.

Even in the face of the undeniable chaos and misery of my life, am I willing to let go, once and for all, of my assumption that I am absolute master of my own existence? Will I give up the illusion that I myself am able in the long run, through sheer effort, to remove all my imperfections and make complete sense out of living through my own resources? Will I become small enough and open up enough to allow the discovery of Reality beyond my understanding or manipulation?

In this way, the discovery of the Higher Power draws a person inescapably to a further step. It is not enough to recognize the greater Reality as real and as saving (Step Two). There is the further question: Will I "turn over" my will and my whole life to the care of "God as I understand God" (Step Three)?

This step is sometimes called surrender. It goes far deeper than mere compliance or obedience to commands. It is fundamentally the act of worship, the unqualified acknowledgment of God as God (in contrast to all forms of "idolatry"), and the entrusting of one's anxious self to this Mystery beyond all grasp.

This kind of surrender springs from the clear recognition of one's desperate condition (Step One) and one's urgent need to be rescued from it by a Higher Power (Step Two). It is a person keenly aware of his or her utter weakness and need who makes this choice to stake everything on the power and goodness of the Mystery.

The spiritual movement of these first three steps is clearly basic and foundational for the recovery of the addicted person. All that follows is a matter of living out the relationship into which one has entered—a process of growing freedom.

The Need for Self-Knowledge

But what are we to say of clergy who have not yet reached the kind of breakdown point that would make them ready for the Twelve Steps? What is their opportunity for spiritual renewal and deepening?

In general, it must come through some kind of honest, realistic look at their spiritual life. Whatever moves a person to that kind of self-examination will lead him or her in the direction of spiritual renewal and growth.

What is crucial, in this connection, is that clergy have someone (or some group) with whom they can speak candidly about their own spiritual condition and needs. To be emotionally isolated and utterly private makes it all too easy to stay a stranger to one's actual state.

Neglecting one's own spiritual condition and needs is, of course, one significant aspect of the general self-neglect that characterizes so many busy and successful clergy. They become so "submerged" in their professional role that they seldom live in a "private" or personal mode.

Professional Spirituality and Personal Spirituality

It may be helpful to distinguish here between professional spirituality and personal spirituality.

It is apparently quite possible for many clergy to live their spiritual lives almost exclusively in the public or communal mode of liturgical prayer, preaching, teaching, and ministering to others. This spirituality might be called professional in the sense of being the official, ecclesial expression of Christian faith. In itself, it is precious—and the clergyperson's expression of it and evoking of it from others is a major part of his or her special ministry to the life of the Body.

On the other hand, a clergyperson who almost completely neglects times of silence, meditation, and personal prayer is very likely to leave his or her own personal relationship to God in the obscure background of awareness.

Clergy who pray only "on the run," in preparation for preaching and other ministry, or with others (in a clerical role) are unlikely to recognize or express their own actual feelings toward God. They tend to relate to God *only* in the role of worship leader and teacher and counselor for others. They do not let their *private pain* or personal struggles be part of their relationship with God.

Also, they hardly ever allow God's uniquely personal leading of their own lives to be perceived. They are not really *listening* to God very much.

Spiritual Dangers for Clergy

This neglect of their own personal spirituality seems closely related to several dangers that threaten almost all clergy.

There is the danger of "pouring out one's cup" of wisdom, inspiration, and encouragement, without ever getting that cup filled up. In the end, there is only an empty cup, with dry dregs at the bottom—and one can begin to perish from thirst.

There is the great danger of being eloquent about the spiritual life for others without living the spiritual life oneself. A good image for this is someone being a kind of referee/coach/guide for others who are participating in some kind of game or treasure hunt, but never playing the game oneself, never seeking or finding any treasure for oneself.

There is the danger of becoming addicted to substances and/or compulsive behaviors in order to escape from the intolerable burden one is carrying and to avoid facing one's own long-buried resentment, emptiness, etc. In fact, we find addictions of one kind or another in the vast majority of our clergy patients.

There is the danger of losing one's own faith (the occupational hazard of the clergy). Because one is so knowledgeable about it all, has all the language down, and comes from "off stage" to make the liturgy happen again and again, there is the awful possibility that it might all become hollow, just the work of one's own mind and hands (for others), with no more power or truth for oneself.

The Need to Share One's Spiritual Life

An important safeguard against all these evils is the practice of sharing one's inner life with certain other people in a very intimate and personal way.

With a trusted friend or, even better, with a circle of trusted peers, one can speak of the joys and sorrows, the fears and temptations, and the urgent struggles of one's own way with God. The circle need not be with fellow clergy, although for some this might be the first option that comes to mind. It can be a great blessing for clergy to be with a circle of laypeople, all members of the one Body, and to both give and receive in a mutual exchange of faith.

With a spiritual director, one can regularly give an account of one's journey, find help in recognizing the leading of the Spirit in one's life, and receive encouragement and counsel for continuing one's spiritual disciplines. In fact, it is scarcely possible to continue very far in the spiritual life without this kind of help.

Spiritual Assessment

All these ways of speaking honestly about one's spiritual life necessarily involve an aspect of self-examination and self-reflection. Hence, it can be very helpful to take a detailed look at one's own spiritual journey and give an account of it to a skilled person who can then reflect it back with interpretation and recommendations for further growth.

At Saint Barnabas we have developed a method for doing a spiritual assessment of our clergy patients (Fehr, 1990). Such an "appreciation" of a spiritual life can help a person to grasp better his or her own personal story with God, a personal "sacred history." Something like this can be done in many settings and especially when first seeking spiritual direction from a wise and experienced person.

The Personal Spirituality of the Professional Minister

A clergyperson's quest for true intimacy with God is a matter of personal spirituality. We might try to specify the meaning of the much-used term *spirituality* as "a concrete way of living in conscious relationship to the mystery of God." The adjective *personal* puts the emphasis on what is specific and unique to an individual. As a matter of fact, each person's story is different, though related to the "great story" that the church keeps telling, generation after generation.

The ordained person needs very much to be aware of his or her own personal story and to honor that. Talking about the "personal spiritual-ity" of the professional minister, moreover, puts the emphasis on that person's humanity and personal needs (so easily neglected or even re-pressed under the pressures of helping others).

The crucial point for the clergyperson to consider is this: Do I *have* a personal life and unique relationship to God? Or am I totally defined by the ministry that I carry out to others?

The tendency for many clergy is to take the second option. This is often bound up with an unhealthy neglect of self and a compulsive, driven caretaking of others.

Anyone who gives priority to this way of living his or her own unique reality will gradually come to discover and appreciate his or her own personal spirituality.

Personal Prayer

Anyone serious about living a spiritual life will devote time to personal prayer, time to relate to God in one's own name, not as official worship leader or minister to others.

What seems to be crucial for spiritual deepening and growth is a discipline of silence. One needs to become outwardly and inwardly quiet, without agenda, in reverent openness to the blessed Mystery.

The most basic attitude of prayer involves settling quietly into one's own center (note the term *centering prayer* currently used to refer to this discipline of silent presence to God). This obviously is closely related to the theme of self-intimacy discussed in an earlier chapter.

In fact, many clergy keep themselves so busy with their ministry to others that they hardly ever settle into quiet presence to themselves (and to God). This is often an avoidance of self-knowledge because of some disorder in one's life that one is reluctant to consider.

At any rate, allowing oneself simply "to be" in God's presence involves, at the same time, being present to self at a deep level. Here there is a close, inseparable connection between seeking intimacy with God and seeking intimacy with self. Values such as self-respect, self-compassion, self-nurture, and self-love are closely related to this stance. It can be a time for a humble but positive self-awareness in relation to the One who loves me.

When one has learned how to enter into this stance, it is possible to "practice" intimacy with God in the sense of being real in relationship to God—recognizing and owning one's feelings toward God, negative as well as positive; trusting that the relationship will not be broken by such emotional honesty.

Here there is a close connection with the theme of interpersonal intimacy, discussed earlier. Learning to be intimate with other human beings is parallel and analogous to learning to be intimate with God. In both kinds of intimacy there is need for trust, so that emotional honesty becomes possible. And with the honesty, the relationship becomes deeper and stronger.

Only in the genuineness of one's relationship to God (entered into again and again, in silence) can one engage in the various forms of prayer—praise, thanksgiving, repentance, petition, intercession, etc. Centering prayer is for many the best way to begin praying because it is simply "becoming present." All prayer forms are richer and deeper ways of relating to God, when they are preceded by centering prayer. This is especially true of liturgical worship and such forms of liturgical prayer as the Office of the Hours.

The Contemplative Attitude

The contemplative attitude toward reality is nourished and grows from the practice of silence and presence. Prior to all asking and all activity is the very mystery of *being*. We need to appreciate the *gift* quality of being, the beauty and mystery of the world. And we need to taste our own being as springing constantly from the creative Love that is God.

For clergy especially, the daily practice of contemplative prayer is bound up with a healthy and much-needed attitude of legitimate self-care. This is the attitude of sabbath, the reverent and joyful celebration of our very life as given to us by God.

Only from that serene and secure ground of our being can we go forth to labor, to be present to others, to be compassionate. Only as we know who we are and to whom we belong, can we engage in ordained ministry without risking self-destruction.

To live out of a contemplative awareness is to have a leisurely approach to the experience of things (instead of always running anxiously to the next commitment). It is also to be attentive to one's own feelings, experiences, desires, needs—honoring the self.

All of this is in contrast to a driven, anxious, even compulsive form of consciousness that is typical of our time and place. As it shows up in the lives of clergy, it often takes the form of overresponsibility and even of the "Messiah complex" analyzed by Rollo May (1938).

Living in Relationship

Grounded in daily silent presence to God, one can *let oneself be loved and affirmed* at the deepest level. Corresponding to the trinitarian mystery of Father, Son, and Spirit, one can let oneself be *creature* (not self-creating or self-validating), *forgiven and beloved sinner* (not self-righteous), and known, forgiven, and loved by others as a *member of the one Body* (not self-sufficient).

In these ways, the primacy of being a person in relationship to other persons (and ultimately to the three-personed God) grounds one's life in love. When rooted and grounded in the security of being lovable and being loved, the most intense and dedicated ministry can be integrated into a healthy human life.

Some positive effects of this kind of spirituality in the life of the minister would be a heightened awareness of God in all things (including the work of ministering to others), a relaxed reliance upon divine power in all that one undertakes, a nonanxious presence to others, a deep *affective* relationship to God, and preaching from the heart *to* the heart.

A Willingness to Be in Process

The spiritual life needs always to be regarded as a process involving many changes, some of which are introduced through much suffering and struggle. In the often quoted words of John Henry Newman, "To live is to change, and to be perfect is to have changed often."

The current language of "being in recovery" seems quite appropriate to the personal spirituality of clergy. In fact, all of us (whether recovering from substance addiction or not) need to understand ourselves as involved in a life-long *process* of transformation.

In the terminology introduced at the beginning of this book, each of us is striving to become the divinely intended "child of God," but this can happen only gradually as we are stripped of the falsehood and evil that distorts our lives, as we come to recognize and affirm our true self, and as we learn to live ever more richly in relationship to one another and to God.

Taking a process view of the spiritual life allows for a compassionate and positive attitude toward self, as well as toward others. Clergy especially need to extend to themselves the same patient, encouraging acceptance they give to others.

Spiritual Needs of Clergy

To develop and maintain a healthy personal spirituality, the clergyperson needs a situation where he or she can regularly be an equal among equals (rather than the spiritual leader of others).

The ordained minister who wishes to live a spiritual life must have a personal spiritual discipline of some kind, a "rule of life" to follow. This must include a period of quiet time each day for being present to God in silent openness.

The clergyperson seeking to grow spiritually will ordinarily need also to work with a spiritual director. It is all too easy for most of us to live our faith in a way that ignores some significant personal issues. The difference between a superficial religiosity and a genuine spiritual life is usually a matter of whether a person is allowing his or her real issues, needs, and problems to be a part of prayer. In particular, each of us needs to face as well as we can our own peculiar temptations and traps.

A good spiritual director will challenge a person who is ignoring or avoiding significant personal realities of life while talking all the while about God.

A Hunger for God

If regarded as duties (what I "really ought to be doing"), all these things will not become established in a person's life. But if one becomes aware of an urgent longing, a hunger and thirst for the living God, then the spiritual activities and disciplines will begin to be felt as precious opportunities.

So there is a certain advantage to being "convicted" of one's spiritual emptiness. Embarrassing as it well may be to the man or woman of God, such spiritual poverty, honestly admitted, can be the starting point for a life-long search for God. In fact, the disposition most open to being blessed and filled is the humble attitude of one who knows that he or she is empty and hungry.

CHAPTER VI

Toward Healthy Integration

What does an emotionally healthy spirituality for clergy look like? From the preceding material, we can draw certain major themes together now into a kind of synthesis.

We begin with the concept of self-care, which is widely recognized today as a basic (though usually neglected) need of clergy. Clergy are continually being exhorted and encouraged to take better care of themselves.

Self-Appreciation and Self-Intimacy

Why do so many of them fail to do so? From our work, it is apparent that many clergy lack the grounding for consistent self-care, namely, a genuine self-appreciation.

We have seen that true intimacy with self involves not only self-knowledge, but also self-appreciation. It means knowing one's own worth, knowing one's strengths and talents as well as one's limitations and weaknesses. In effect, self-appreciation is included in the virtue of *humility*, understood as the recognition and acceptance of the *truth* about oneself before God.

Where does healthy self-appreciation come from? It is clear that it cannot be acquired in self-sufficient isolation. Developmentally, it arises out of being respected and affirmed by others from our earliest years. Long before anyone can say "I" with self-confidence and self-esteem, he or she has been addressed lovingly countless times as "you" by parents and other adults.

But persons who did not get enough of this affirmation by others early in life wind up struggling against a sense of inner void. Many clergy, it appears, suffer from this kind of deficit.

Clergy, like others in helping professions, often do their best to be good for others as a way of earning self-esteem. But no amount of admirable and successful ministry to others manages to fill the gaping void within.

At the same time, most clergy are relatively isolated, emotionally and spiritually, without enough *peer* support. They stand alone, as helpers to others, but are not appreciated or affirmed as equals.

For such clergy, what is essential to the "recovery" of self-esteem— as a solid basis for living—is their relationship with others and ultimately with God.

The Need for Community

Participating in a genuine spiritual community as an equal is very impor- tant for a cleric's health and well-being. Clergy, like other human be- ings, need to be known and loved in a circle of face-to-face relationships with peers. They often do not have this kind of community participation even though they stand as the facilitators and focal points of Christian community for their congregations.

The need is to be honest about one's own life, to give and receive affection, to give and receive forgiveness, and to express one's personal faith and faith-struggles. In the long run, no one—clergy or lay—can live a healthy spiritual life without that kind of a life-context for his or her journey.

Clergy who recognize that they are relatively isolated need to take the initiative to find or create the kind of peer spiritual community in which they can live and grow.

Groups

In this connection, we recommend group work or interaction as a place for clergy to begin to relate on personal levels. Something can be learned from the current men's movement, which recognizes men's need to gather in groups to do their grief-work over the common loss of fathering in our culture. The argument is made convincingly that when men learn to have certain fathering and mentoring needs met by other men, there is reduced likelihood of men turning to women in hopes that they will satisfy these needs. Such men's-group work, outside the parish, can help those clergy who tend to turn to female parishioners for "mothering," which leads to further boundary confusions as genital sexuality enters in.

Group work would seem to be equally important for female clergy, who must overcome discrimination and various hurdles, in order to serve in the church. Many of them are single, too. They need to form associations and groups in which they can give one another much-needed appreciation, affirmation, and encouragement.

Intimacy with Others

Through group work clergy can learn to relate in the ways of true interpersonal intimacy. It is crucial for clergy to develop and keep relationships that are personal, not professionally related. This means relationships in which they are not functioning in their role or professional responsibilities.

Without such personal relationships, they are in danger of knowing only how to relate to others in their role. One seasoned pastor, for example, confided in us that he knew more about being a pastor than about being a person.

This, of course, raises the problem of parishioners as intimate companions. For those connected with the church, clergy are always perceived as in role; they have some recognized responsibility and professional boundaries. The key phrase for understanding the kind of relationships needed for health is *out of role and responsibility*.

Marriage

One might think this would point toward the spouse, a person one could relate to person-to-person, out of role and professional responsibility. Sadly, however, the typical female clergy-spouse has been too much involved with his work in the church, and the male clergy too much invested in bringing the authority of his role home, for this to work out.

Surveys find the female clergy-spouse falling into a confidential, therapist-like role as recipient of her ordained husband's disclosed feelings and thoughts aroused by his job-related stories and stresses. Clergy list their spouses first, above their bishops, as those to whom they first turn for support and encouragement for job-related stressors. This often deteriorates into a one-way relationship, with the female clergy-spouse acting as a kind of "ear" for her husband.

This kind of spousal role expectation is too much connected with the primacy of the male ministerial role. In such a relationship, there is a loss of equality and mutuality. Moreover, this spousal role too often results in enmeshment wherein the female clergy-spouse becomes engulfed in the husband's ministerial career.

In this regard, many parish-pastor working conditions and arrangements put the spouse and the rest of the family at risk. The family's housing, church-relationship, and reputation all hang on his job performance and conduct. His job failure and termination cost the family more than the average nonordained person's job loss.

There are signs of positive change as female clergy-spouses locate their own pastors other than their spouses. Some are even attending different churches altogether. Such arrangements, while threatening to some male pastors and congregations, are steps in the right direction and keep the marital relationship open to being more personal and less stuck in his role and profession.

Friendships

Where to look for personal, out-of-role relationships? We believe they should be with peers—other adults. Some possibilities are those in allied helping professions and clergy and laity of other faith-traditions. Friendships with such persons can have a more personal and trusting quality, and both parties can speak freely of their work pressures and concerns without fear of violations of confidences.

The question arises as to whether such personal relationships are to be with same-sex or opposite-sex friends. Intimacy knows no bounds of gender, but we are not all able at any given time in our lives to distinguish both in impact and intention the boundary between intimacy and genitality.

To have an intimate relationship with a person of the same gender as one's sexual preference is possible to the extent one can distinguish both in inner dynamics and in practice the boundaries as described in earlier chapters between intimacy and genitality.

This is an area for caution and an arena fraught with possibilities for self-deception. Such a relationship, if nurtured, needs the help of an outside, objective person, a therapist or spiritual director. Once genitality enters such a relationship where intimacy alone had been, then the particular relationship is changed significantly, and the other arenas of intimacy, with self and with God, are altered and confused.

For most of us, most of the time, it is recommended that intimate relationships such as we are prescribing be limited to those of the opposite gender of our sexual preference, so as to help us experience more clearly the boundaries between our need for intimacy and our need for genitality.

It has been our experience and observation that when clergy needs for intimacy have been realized and nurtured, then their sexual and genital needs also become more a matter of free choice, less driven and compulsive. These needs are also less likely to be confused with the needs for power and achievement, as in the cases of pastoral sexual abuse of parishioners. Without such intimate relationships as described here, clergy become vulnerable to acting out in unhealthy and dangerous ways.

Intimacy with God

As we have seen, the ultimate grounding of self-appreciation must be found in one's relationship to God. So, intimacy with God is really the indispensable accompaniment of true intimacy with self.

This is a matter of major importance for clergy health and wholeness. It certainly may not be taken for granted that a clergyperson is living in true intimacy with God just because he or she is carrying out effectively the duties of pastor to others.

As we have seen, there is need to develop and cultivate a personal spirituality. There is a need for a heartfelt personal relationship with God, into which one enters ever more deeply each day.

The Need for Integration

Many clergy are suffering from a lack of integration in their lives. Typically, as we have seen, there is a split-off "public self" (the facade or "glittering image") that they maintain through great effort, with the intellect dominant. Their lifestyle is one of *control* and, in a sense, of image management.

Such people are not aware of their own feelings nor do they have access to their own "depths" (their past, their hurts and resentments, their needs for nurture, etc.).

Their lives might be characterized by the *split* between head and heart, public and private, professional and personal.

Poverty of Spirit

The beginning of the healing of this split, as we have seen, is in the acknowledgment of one's pain and the "unmanageability" of one's life. In spiritual terms, this is the recognition of true "poverty of spirit," of one's utter neediness and dependence upon the bounty of God's grace.

There is a biblical text that might well be taken as the pattern for the kind of conversion that such clergy need. In Revelation 3, the risen Lord sends this message to the believers in Laodicea:

> You say, "I am rich, I have prospered, and I need nothing." You do not realize that you are wretched, pitiable, poor, blind, and naked. Therefore, I counsel you to buy from me gold refined by fire so that you may be rich; and white robes to clothe you and keep the shame of your nakedness from being seen; and salve to anoint your eyes so that you may see. I reprove and discipline those whom I love. Be earnest, therefore, and repent. Listen! I am standing at the door, knocking; if you hear my voice and open the door, I will come in to you and eat with you, and you with me (Rev. 3:17-20).

In this text the dimensions of intimacy with self and intimacy with God are clearly expressed. Intimacy with others is not explicit but perhaps implied in the image of the Eucharistic feast.

The entry into what we have been calling recovery is here depicted as the recognition of utter *need* (under the images of being poor, blind, and naked). Until one reaches this point of truth (humility), he or she cannot yet begin to accept the riches of Grace. Hence, a true estimate of one's actual condition (self-intimacy) is required.

But what follows goes even beyond the remedying of the recognized state of need (receiving gold, eye-ointment, and white garments). The decisive gift is nothing less than the intimacy with God that is actually every human being's greatest need and ultimate destiny. The image of opening the door of the self (in response to Christ's patient, respectful knocking) leads then to the image of sitting at table with Him—the greatest possible intimacy. (And, as suggested, if one takes the Eucharistic image in its full meaning, there is also the dimension of communion and intimacy with others.)

The Movement toward Intimacy

In Diagram 6, we attempt to summarize in one schematic overview the various possibilities of health and unhealth in terms of the three levels of intimacy. "Health and salvation" (to use a liturgical phrase) are to be found in the movement toward Quadrant I (where there is simultaneously a maximum of both personal power and relationship).

This movement is a matter of (1) increasing self-discovery and self-appreciation (and the corresponding increase of personal power), (2) more and more healthy, satisfying relationships with others, and (3) ever more intimate relationship with God.

These three spheres of intimacy are, of course, inseparable. Self-appreciation is grounded in the love and appreciation received from other human beings in relationships and most profoundly in the gratuitous, affirming creative Love that God is. Hence, self-appreciation cannot be attained in isolation, but only by opening oneself increasingly to these interpersonal relationships.

On the other hand, true intimacy with others is made more and more possible and actual to the extent that self-appreciation and self-intimacy increases. In the biblical phrase, we can love our neighbors only *as* we love ourselves. And our ability to be passionately intimate with God grows also as we learn to honor all the dimensions and feelings of the self.

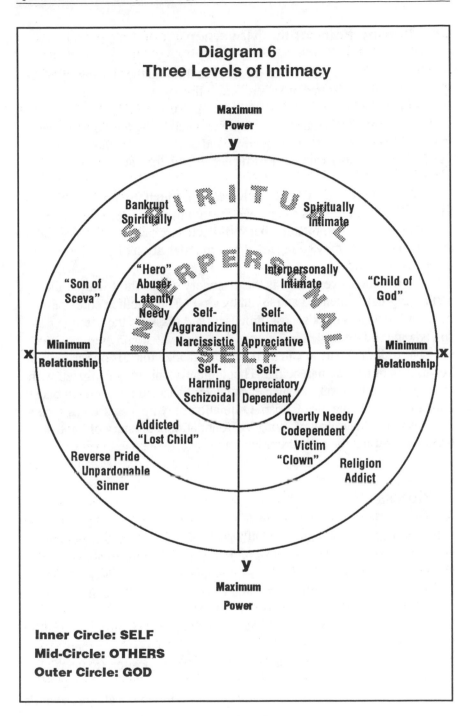

Diagram 6
Three Levels of Intimacy

Maximum
Power
y

SPIRITUAL

INTERPERSONAL

SELF

Bankrupt
Spiritually

Spiritually
Intimate

"Son of
Sceva"

"Hero"
Abuser
Latently
Needy

Interpersonally
Intimate

"Child of
God"

Self-
Aggrandizing
Narcissistic

Self-
Intimate
Appreciative

Minimum
Relationship
x

Self-
Harming
Schizoidal

Self-
Depreciatory
Dependent

Minimum
Relationship
x

Addicted
"Lost Child"

Overtly Needy
Codependent
Victim
"Clown"

Reverse Pride
Unpardonable
Sinner

Religion
Addict

y
Maximum
Power

Inner Circle: SELF
Mid-Circle: OTHERS
Outer Circle: GOD

The Starting Point of the Movement

As already noted, the entry into recovery is through the "narrow gate" of genuine humility. To move toward real intimacy with self, others, and God, I must begin by facing the reality of my life.

For clergy, this means recognizing and accepting their own *human- ity*—with the mixed legacy of positive and negative elements from the family of origin, and with their own checkered personal history of sin and grace.

To do this is often a matter of breaking through the shame barrier. This can happen only in a supportive community of peers, where one is loved and affirmed no matter what self-disclosure occurs. Theologically, such a community may be regarded as a manifestation of the mystery of the Body of Christ.

What results, eventually, is the discovery of the child-within, the self as originally intended and loved by God. This "golden core" be- neath all the layers of falseness, defenses, and masks is the genuine per- son whom God loves.

The ordained person can then come to realize that his or her first vocation is to be a human being. Theologically, this may be linked with the mystery of baptism in which each person is called uniquely by his or her name and claimed for Christ. Ordination may then be seen as secon- dary, as a particular way of living the foundational mystery of baptism (one's vocation to be a "child of God").

In Process

When the true self or "child of God" has been discovered, the wonderful surprise is that this self is *good enough* (that is, quite acceptable in God's sight). This allows for humble self-acceptance and for an honest, patient life of growth and learning, of gradual recovery from all the distortions caused by "original sin" and personal sin.

As noted earlier, a *process* view of the human condition is liberating for the recovering person. To live "in recovery" can be seen, then, as an ongoing process of claiming and living one's first vocation (to be a human being) with more and more integrity.

None of this, of course, is in any contradiction to the clergy person's further vocation to be ordained minister for the Body. Rather, he or she will become increasingly fruitful in this special vocation insofar as he or she grows more healthy and integrated as a human being.

Living out one's primary vocation, to be a human being, involves many aspects of self-intimacy. We touch now on a few more of these.

One's Body

For all their talk of the body as a temple of the Holy Spirit, many clergy actually ignore or even harm their bodies. Such clergy live in their heads, cerebrally and theoretically.

They need to learn how to "listen" to their bodies' messages. For example, they need to notice when they are tired and in need of rest or to recognize the bodily presentations of their various feelings, how their bodies react when they are angry or sad.

Alienation from one's own body, in fact, has a close parallel in being "out of touch" with one's feelings. To be intimate with oneself means also to be able to discern affective states. Simply expressed, this means knowing when one is angry, sad, hurt, ashamed, glad, or afraid. So many clergy know only, if at all, that they are "upset" and that they should ignore it. This inability to name feelings has been described in chapters I and II.

Male clergy, as males, are especially prone to regard their bodies as machines for work and/or pleasure, rather than appreciating their bodies as integrated aspects of their selves. Most male clergy tend to use their bodies as machines for work, which they expect to run and operate more than sixteen hours a day. Food becomes fuel for this machine, "pumped in" fast and on the run, so as to attempt to eke out of this machine all its possible energy and resources. All this, of course, in the name of a dubious asceticism and the heroic call to ministry.

Women's relationship to their bodies tends to be more incarnational. Female clergy are more likely to appreciate their bodies, not as work or pleasure machines but as integrated shelters designed to bear and nurture new life. From menarche to menopause, women's experience of body is integrated as something happening to them on a monthly basis, a process they can neither control nor manipulate. It is a process connected with a mystery of life that women must ultimately accept and to which they must simply surrender. Men, denied this kind of bodily experience, are more likely to imagine that they can control, use, and turn their bodies off and on at will.

Bodies are what we are, not what we have. We are our bodies; bodies are ourselves. Intimacy with self, therefore, means acceptance and appreciation of one's body. Care of self includes care of body. This includes some regular exercise, physical exams, and the elimination of harmful habits such as smoking and eating fats. Clergy are not exempt from the need to cultivate good health habits and cannot justify harmful habits by appealing to some sort of asceticism or the demands of ministry.

On the other hand, clergy are committed to interpersonal and spiritual levels of intimacy beyond focusing on the self and its bodily aspects. They must avoid the cult of health, beauty, and fitness so prominent in our day, with its near exclusive emphasis on looks and physique. This cult not only equates self-intimacy with the proper nurturing of one's physique, but it is also out of touch with the interpersonal and spiritual struggles involved in the achievement of intimacy in all its dimensions.

Use of Food

On a very elementary level, some clergy abuse food, not just in using it as fuel for their body-machines, but in the quality and quantity of what they eat. To regard eating habits as irrelevant to one's spiritual life is typical of the Western mentality of mind-body dualism.

In contrast to this, one author recalls attending a yoga retreat center where, after stating that he was dedicated to living out a disciplined spiritual life, he was asked, "What do you eat?" This unexpected and humbling question brought home the basic connection between diet and spiritual welfare, the wholistic and vital connectedness of one's "care of body, care of soul" as unified realities under our enfleshed human condition.

One's Past

Intimacy with oneself also has a historical perspective. To know one's personal and generational past becomes a critical element. To look squarely at one's family of origin legacies, limitations, and tendencies is to be aware and alive, and many times to be in considerable pain. To challenge a myth and to reexamine what really went on at home is a process of considerable moment and pain, for some almost a rebirth. The loyalty and quasi-identity attachment to mythical parents runs deep and occasions much de-illusionment if not outright disillusionment in those who are forced to challenge their naive assumptions. Yet, there is no other way to become a separate self, free and capable of intimacy.

For some the problem of forgiveness arises. Many clergy forgive too quickly, without feeling the pain or taking an account of the price they paid for their parents' mistakes or abuse. Others feel unreasonable guilt as they cannot manage to forgive the abuse they suffered. They heap more shame and guilt upon themselves for not being forgiving. We recall that Jesus on the cross did not say "*I* forgive you." He prayed instead to his Father to do the forgiveness. "Father, forgive them." In any case, the emotional letting-go and moving-ahead is the more important aspect of forgiveness.

Time

Finally, relationship to oneself has also to do with time. This is an aspect of life that has gotten out of proportion for many clergy.

Time is life, and life is more than ministerial tasks. Many unhealthy clergy work too much and too long. Whether driven by the "Messiah complex," by the simple inability to ask for help or to delegate, or by a compulsive attention to trivial details, clergy avoid their inner emptiness and poverty of spirit by overworking their weekly hours, often in unprofessional busy-work or work outside their hiring agreement.

On the practical level, some facts may be helpful. A clergyperson who has one full day off and away weekly, plus four weeks of vacation and seven paid holidays, has only seventy-nine days off per year. In contrast, the parishioner who works full-time usually gets two days off weekly, but even with only two weeks of vacation and seven paid holidays, this person has a total of 121 days off per year. That's a difference of forty-two days! Surely, the clergyperson can legitimately take some extra time for nurturing self-intimacy: continuing education, retreats, weekly gatherings for sharing, etc.

If we regard time in a spiritual perspective, it becomes important to recognize that it is a *gift*. We do not simply possess time in any absolute sense but are, rather, stewards of it. To speak of "*my*" time in the sense of strict ownership is really a misnomer, a false premise, and a spiritual delusion.

Time is to be enjoyed gratefully and used responsibly. It is an ever-renewed, incalculable opportunity to live in the present moment. There is much wisdom in the recovery movement's stress on "one day at a time," in contrast to an unlimited notion of time as unending and ever available. In reality, we do not have "all the time in the world" to squander as we seek to achieve our true destiny, "what God intends" for our lives. We need to be good stewards of the time that God entrusts to us.

Regarding the present moment always as a gift of God could have a salutary effect on a clergyperson's organization of life. Healthy intimacy with self would allow for sabbath time, time simply to be, to enjoy, to be in relationships, to pray. It would also allow for limited and reasonable periods of time to work and minister to others.

Conclusion

To name the features of a healthy spirituality for clergy is, to be sure, not enough. To actually *live out* any or all of the ideals sketched in this chapter is, for anyone, a matter of Grace and the day-by-day, creative process of living.

On the other hand, we hope it may be of service to our fellow clergy to have delineated clearly the themes that emerge from our clinical work. To see both the patterns of unhealth and the ways of healing and recovery could be a powerful incentive to do something about one's own state of health.

Our intention has been to offer insight and encouragement to the working clergy of our churches and to all those who collaborate with and minister to them. If this little book helps any of its readers to a more healthy and integrated life of ministry, it will have served its purpose.

EPILOGUE

We, the authors, conclude our written work with a prayer that our readers come away with more strength than solace, more resolve than resolutions. We have worked with some four hundred clergy; most fell short of their ideals and yet discovered God's awkward Grace at work even in the valleys and pits of their lives. Such an experience leaves us strengthened, encouraged, and resolved. We hope we have communicated something of this to you, our readers, whom we may never meet or know. Broken promises and failed ideals do not mean that promises and ideals should not be made and remade. We are impressed by the courage and faith of our patients who have reached out in their time of darkness and loss, who have admitted their mistakes and failures, sometimes reluctantly, but who have also clung to the unconditional love of God who radically accepts them not only in spite of but even with all their brokenness and shame. Such faith has kept many from total despair and suicide. We are the better for having had the privilege of knowing these lives so intimately. The journey toward health and salvation is available to us all. We end by joining our readers as fellow journeyers on the way.

BIBLIOGRAPHY

Alcoholics Anonymous: The Story of How Many Thousands of Men and Women Have Recovered from Alcoholism. 3d ed. New York: Alcoholics Anonymous World Services, 1976.

Berne, Eric. *Games People Play.* New York: Grove Press, 1964.

Bolt, Robert. *A Man for All Seasons.* London: Heinemann, 1960.

Carnes, Patrick. *Contrary to Love.* Minneapolis: CompCare, 1989.

Erikson, Erik. *Childhood and Society.* New York: Norton, 1963.

Fehr, Wayne L. "The Spiritual Assessment of Clergy in Crisis." *Action Information* (June-July 1990): 6-8.

Fox, Matthew. *Original Blessing.* Santa Fe: Bear & Co., 1983.

Hands, Donald R. "Co-Dependency: Clinically, Clerically and Congregationally." *Action Information* (September-October 1990): 15-17.

_____. "Toward Liberation from Shamed Sexuality." *Action Information* (May-June 1991): 29-33.

Howatch, Susan. *Glittering Images.* New York: Fawcett Crest, 1987.

Jung, Carl G. "The Stages of Life." In *The Portable Jung,* edited by Joseph Campbell, 3-22. New York: The Viking Press, 1971.

Kaufman, Gershen. *Shame: The Power of Caring.* Rochester, VT: Schenkman Books, 1980, 1985.

May, Gerald. *The Awakened Heart*. San Francisco: Harper, 1991.

May, Rollo. *The Art of Counseling*. Nashville: Abingdon Press, 1938.

_____. *Love and Will*. New York: W. W. Norton & Co., 1969.

_____. *Power and Innocence*. New York: W. W. Norton & Co., 1972.

Sullivan, Harry Stack. *The Interpersonal Theory of Psychiatry*. New York: W. W. Norton & Co., 1953.